ENGLISH
FOR EVERYONE
LIBRO DE EJERCICIOS
NIVEL **2** INICIAL

AUDIO GRATUITO
web y app
www.dkefe.com

Autor

Thomas Booth ha trabajado durante 10 años como profesor de inglés en Polonia y en Rusia. Actualmente vive en Inglaterra, donde trabaja como editor y autor de materiales para el aprendizaje de la lengua inglesa, principalmente manuales y vocabularios.

Consultor del curso

Tim Bowen ha enseñado inglés y ha formado profesores en más de 30 países en todo el mundo. Es coautor de libros sobre la enseñanza de la pronunciación y sobre la metodología de la enseñanza de idiomas, y autor de numerosos libros para profesores de inglés. Actualmente se dedica a la escritura de materiales, la edición y la traducción.
Es miembro del Chartered Institute of Linguists.

Consultora lingüística

La profesora **Susan Barduhn** cuenta con una gran experiencia en la enseñanza del inglés y la formación de profesores. Como autora ha participado en numerosas publicaciones. Además de dirigir cursos de inglés en cuatro continentes, ha sido presidenta de la Asociación Internacional de Profesores de Inglés como Lengua Extranjera y asesora del British Council y del Departamento de Estado de Estados Unidos. Actualmente es profesora de la School for International Training en Vermont, Estados Unidos.

ENGLISH
FOR EVERYONE

LIBRO DE EJERCICIOS

NIVEL 2 INICIAL

DK India
Edición sénior Vineetha Mokkil, Anita Kakar
Edición de arte sénior Chhaya Sajwan
Edición del proyecto Antara Moitra
Edición Agnibesh Das, Nisha Shaw, Seetha Natesh
Edición de arte Namita, Heena Sharma, Sukriti Sobti,
Shipra Jain, Aanchal Singhal
Asistencia editorial Ira Pundeer, Ateendriya Gupta,
Sneha Sunder Benjamin, Ankita Yadav
Asistencia de edición de arte Roshni Kapur,
Meenal Goel, Priyansha Tuli
Ilustración Ivy Roy, Arun Pottirayil, Bharti Karakoti, Rahul Kumar
Búsqueda de imágenes Deepak Negi
Dirección editorial Pakshalika Jayaprakash
Dirección de la edición de arte Arunesh Talapatra
Dirección de producción Pankaj Sharma
Dirección de preproducción Balwant Singh
Diseño sénior DTP Vishal Bhatia, Neeraj Bhatia
Diseño DTP Sachin Gupta
Diseño de cubierta Surabhi Wadhwa
Dirección editorial de cubierta Saloni Singh
Diseño sénior DTP (cubierta) Harish Aggarwal

DK Reino Unido
Asistencia editorial Jessica Cawthra, Sarah Edwards
Ilustración Edwood Burn, Denise Joos,
Michael Parkin, Jemma Westing
Producción de audio Liz Hammond
Dirección editorial Daniel Mills
Dirección de la edición de arte Anna Hall
Dirección del proyecto Christine Stroyan
Diseño de cubierta Natalie Godwin
Edición de cubierta Claire Gell
Dirección de desarrollo del diseño de cubierta Sophia MTT
Producción, preproducción Luca Frassinetti
Producción Mary Slater
Dirección de la edición Andrew Macintyre
Dirección de arte Karen Self
Dirección general editorial Jonathan Metcalf

De la edición española
Coordinación editorial Lakshmi Asensio
Asistencia editorial y producción Eduard Sepúlveda

Publicado originalmente en Gran Bretaña en 2016
por Dorling Kindersley Limited. DK, One Embassy Gardens,
8 Viaduct Gardens, London SW11 7BW
Parte de Penguin Random House

Título original: *English For Everyone. Practice Book. Level 2. Beginner*
Segunda reimpresión: 2024

Contenidos

Cómo funciona el curso

English for Everyone está pensado para todas aquellas personas que quieren aprender inglés por su cuenta. Como cualquier curso de idiomas, cubre las habilidades básicas: gramática, vocabulario, pronunciación, escucha, conversación, lectura y escritura.

A diferencia de otros cursos, todo ello se practica y aprende de forma enormemente visual, con el apoyo de gráficos e imágenes que te ayudarán a entender y a recordar. Los ejercicios de este volumen están pensados para consolidar lo aprendido en el libro de estudio. Sigue las unidades por orden y utiliza al máximo los audios disponibles en la web y la app.

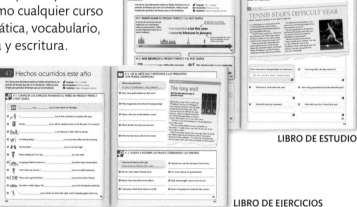

LIBRO DE ESTUDIO

LIBRO DE EJERCICIOS

Número de unidad Este libro está dividido en unidades. En cada una de ellas se practica lo aprendido en la misma unidad del libro de estudio.

Qué vas a practicar La unidad comienza con un resumen de lo que practicarás en ella.

Módulos Cada unidad se compone de distintos módulos que debes seguir por orden. Puedes tomarte un descanso tras completar cualquiera de ellos.

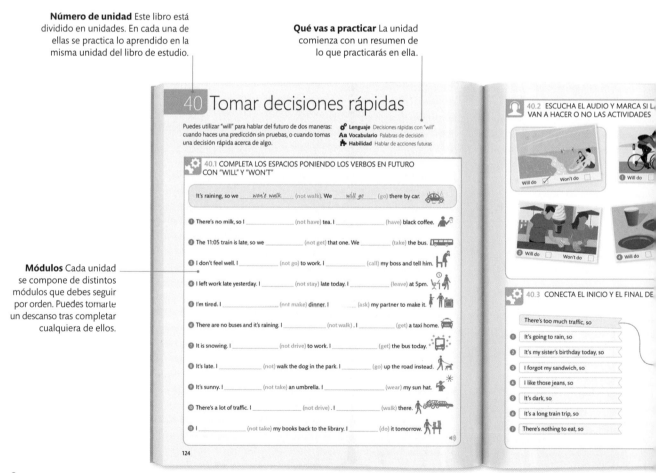

Vocabulario Las páginas de vocabulario ponen a prueba tu memoria sobre las palabras y las expresiones clave que has aprendido en el libro de estudio.

Guía visual Imágenes y gráficos te dan pistas visuales que te ayudan a fijar en la memoria las palabras más importantes.

17 Vocabulario

Aa 17.1 **GEOGRAFÍA** ESCRIBE LAS PALABRAS DEL RECUADRO BAJO SU IMAGEN

rocks	coast	swamp		cave	woods	desert	oasis
sand dune		river	polar region	valley	mountain	rainforest	canyon
iceberg	beach	waterfall		pond	island	cliff	hill

57

Audio de apoyo La mayoría de los módulos cuentan con audio grabado por hablantes nativos que te ayudará a mejorar tu expresión y tu comprensión.

AUDIO GRATUITO
web y app
www.dkefe.com

Módulos de ejercicios

Cada ejercicio está cuidadosamente graduado para que profundices y contrastes lo que has aprendido en la unidad. Si haces los ejercicios a medida que avanzas, asimilarás y recordarás mejor los conceptos, y tu inglés será más fluido. Cada ejercicio indica con un símbolo qué habilidad vas a practicar con él.

GRAMÁTICA
Aplica las nuevas reglas en distintos contextos.

LECTURA
Analiza ejemplos del idioma en textos reales en inglés.

ESCUCHA
Comprueba tu comprensión del inglés hablado.

VOCABULARIO
Consolida tu comprensión del vocabulario clave.

CONVERSACIÓN
Compara tu dicción con los audios de muestra.

Número de módulo Cada módulo tiene su propio número, para que te sea fácil localizar las respuestas y el audio correspondiente.

Instrucciones En cada ejercicio tienes unas breves instrucciones que te dicen qué debes hacer.

Ayuda gráfica
Las ilustraciones te ayudan a entender los ejercicios.

Audio de apoyo Este símbolo indica que las respuestas a los ejercicios están disponibles en grabaciones de audio. Escúchalas tras completar el ejercicio.

Espacio para escribir Es útil que escribas las respuestas en el libro, pues te servirán para repasar lo aprendido.

Respuesta de ejemplo
La primera respuesta ya está escrita, para que entiendas mejor el ejercicio.

Ejercicios de escucha Este símbolo te avisa de que debes escuchar el audio para poder responder a las preguntas.

Ejercicio de conversación
Este símbolo indica que debes decir las respuestas en voz alta y compararlas a continuación con su audio correspondiente.

Audio

English for Everyone incorpora abundantes materiales en audio. Te recomendamos que los utilices al máximo, pues te ayudarán a mejorar tu comprensión del inglés hablado y a lograr una pronunciación y un acento más naturales. Escucha cada audio tantas veces como quieras. Páusalo y vuelve atrás en los pasajes que te resulten difíciles, hasta que estés seguro de que has entendido bien lo que se dice.

EJERCICIOS DE ESCUCHA
Este símbolo indica que debes escuchar el audio a fin de poder responder las preguntas del ejercicio.

AUDIO DE APOYO
Este símbolo indica que dispones de audios adicionales que puedes escuchar tras completar el módulo.

AUDIO GRATUITO
web y app
www.dkefe.com

Respuestas

Al final del libro tienes una sección con las respuestas correctas de todos los ejercicios. Consúltala al terminar cada módulo y compara tus respuestas con los ejemplos para comprobar si has entendido bien los contenidos que has estado practicando.

11

11.1
1 I **am not** feeling well today, I'm sorry. Let's meet next week instead.
2 May and Clara are **feeling** sick today. They're going to stay at home.
3 Cathy **isn't** feeling well. She is not going swimming today.
4 Jerry is **feeling** really sick, but he's still going to work.
5 We don't **feel** well, so we aren't coming to the party tonight.
6 Alexander **isn't** feel well. He's going to stay at home today.
7 They don't **feel** well. They're not going to visit their uncle and aunt today.
8 Hilary isn't **feeling** well. She can't come to the movies tonight.
9 Lee **feels** sick. He can't come to the sales meeting today.
10 John and Diana **are** not feeling well. They are going to leave work early today.

Respuestas Tienes las respuestas de todos los ejercicios al final del libro.

11.2
1 I can't hear and I have an earache.
2 Dan's leg hurts.
3 Maria has a broken leg.
4 I don't feel well. I have a stomachache.
5 Claire has a terrible headache.
6 I have a pain in my knee.
7 Philip can't stand. He has backache.

Audio Este símbolo indica que puedes escuchar el audio de las respuestas.

11.3
1 False 2 True 3 False 4 True
5 Not given 6 True 7 False

Número de ejercicio Para que las localices más fácilmente, las respuestas indican el número del ejercicio.

11.4
1. I have a broken leg.
2. I have a pain in my foot.
3. I have a headache.
4. I have got a broken leg.
5. I have got a pain in my foot.
6. I have got a headache.
7. You have got a broken leg.
8. You have got a headache.
9. You have a broken leg.
10. You have a headache.
11. Anna has a broken leg.
12. Anna has a headache.

01 Hablar sobre ti

Cuando quieres hablarle a alguien sobre ti, o sobre personas o asuntos relacionados contigo, usas la forma del present simple de "to be".

⚙ **Lenguaje** Utilizar "to be"
Aa Vocabulario Nombres, profesiones y familia
🧩 **Habilidad** Hablar sobre ti

1.1 TACHA LA PALABRA INCORRECTA DE CADA FRASE

Jack ~~are~~ / is 27 years old.

1. They are / is the Walker family.
2. You am / are a police officer.
3. Eve is / are from Canada.
4. I is / am a teacher.
5. We are / is Australian.
6. He am / is an artist.

🔊

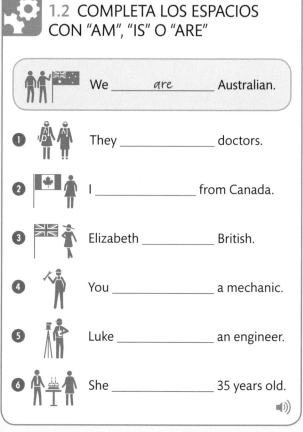

1.2 COMPLETA LOS ESPACIOS CON "AM", "IS" O "ARE"

We ____are____ Australian.

1. They _____ doctors.
2. I _____ from Canada.
3. Elizabeth _____ British.
4. You _____ a mechanic.
5. Luke _____ an engineer.
6. She _____ 35 years old.

🔊

1.3 UTILIZA EL DIAGRAMA PARA CREAR OCHO FRASES CORRECTAS Y DILAS EN VOZ ALTA

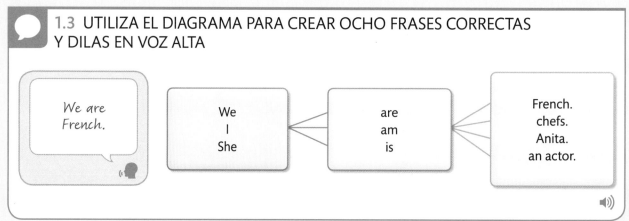

We are French.

| We / I / She | are / am / is | French. / chefs. / Anita. / an actor. |

🔊

1.4 COMPLETA LOS ESPACIOS PARA FORMAR FRASES NEGATIVAS

I ___am not___ from Argentina.

1. John and Ellie _____ best friends.
2. Mr. Robbins _____ a teacher.
3. It _____ 2 o'clock.
4. You _____ my sister.
5. Annabelle _____ at school.
6. Ann and Ravi _____ students.
7. Ken _____ a mechanic.
8. We _____ doctors.
9. He _____ 45 years old.
10. They _____ my teachers.
11. She _____ from Ireland.
12. It _____ Martha's book.

🔊

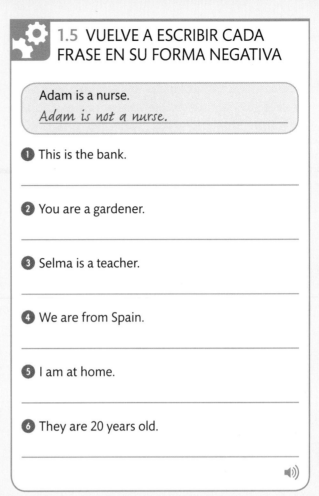

1.5 VUELVE A ESCRIBIR CADA FRASE EN SU FORMA NEGATIVA

Adam is a nurse.
Adam is not a nurse.

1. This is the bank.
_____

2. You are a gardener.
_____

3. Selma is a teacher.
_____

4. We are from Spain.
_____

5. I am at home.
_____

6. They are 20 years old.
_____

🔊

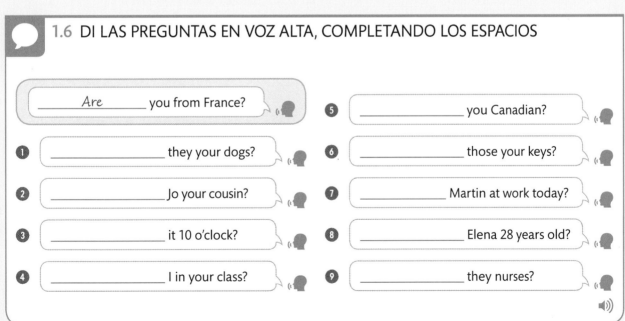

1.6 DI LAS PREGUNTAS EN VOZ ALTA, COMPLETANDO LOS ESPACIOS

___Are___ you from France?

1. _____ they your dogs?
2. _____ Jo your cousin?
3. _____ it 10 o'clock?
4. _____ I in your class?
5. _____ you Canadian?
6. _____ those your keys?
7. _____ Martin at work today?
8. _____ Elena 28 years old?
9. _____ they nurses?

🔊

02 Hablar sobre rutinas

Puedes utilizar frases en present simple para hablar de tus rutinas diarias, aficiones y tus pertenencias. Utiliza "do" para formar frases negativas y preguntas.

⚙ **Lenguaje** Present simple
Aa Vocabulario Rutinas y aficiones
Habilidad Hablar de tus rutinas

2.1 TACHA LA PALABRA INCORRECTA DE CADA FRASE

Eddie ~~live~~ / **lives** in Canada.

❶ They **cook** / **cooks** pizza for dinner.

❷ Your friend **has** / **have** a microwave.

❸ She **work** / **works** at the gym.

❹ I **watch** / **watches** TV every day.

❺ We **leaves** / **leave** work at 5pm.

❻ Mark **has** / **have** a skateboard.

❼ They **start** / **starts** school at 9am.

❽ You **hates** / **hate** soccer.

❾ Tara **eat** / **eats** breakfast at 7:15am.

❿ I **go** / **goes** to the park after work.

⓫ We **wakes up** / **wake up** at 7am.

⓬ He **cook** / **cooks** dinner at 8pm.

⓭ My son **walks** / **walk** to school.

🔊

2.2 COMPLETA LOS ESPACIOS CON LAS PALABRAS DEL RECUADRO

 We ____*live*____ in New York.

❶ Laura _____ TV all day.

❷ You _____ at 7am.

❸ I _____ work at 6pm.

❹ My cousins _____ to the gym.

❺ She _____ a laptop.

❻ James _____ in a bank.

❼ They _____ lunch at 1:30pm.

| has | ~~live~~ | go | wake up | watches | leave | eat | works |

🔊

2.3 DI LAS FRASES EN VOZ ALTA, COMPLETANDO LOS ESPACIOS

Omar __works__ (work) in an office.

1. They _____ (eat) pizza for lunch.

2. Mia _____ (get up) late on Saturdays.

3. You _____ (go) to work early.

4. We _____ (cook) dinner at 7:30pm.

5. Paul _____ (finish) work at 6pm.

6. Lily _____ (watch) TV every day.

7. They _____ (start) work at 10am.

8. Robert _____ (have) a car.

9. I _____ (wake up) at 6:45am.

10. Jay _____ (study) science every day.

11. Karen _____ (like) tennis.

12. He _____ (work) in a school.

13. Jess _____ (go) to bed at 10pm.

2.4 ESCUCHA EL AUDIO Y NUMERA LAS IMÁGENES EN EL ORDEN EN QUE SE DESCRIBEN

A ☐   B ☐ 1   C ☐

D ☐   E ☐   F ☐

2.5 LEE EL BLOG Y RESPONDE A LAS PREGUNTAS

Edward lives in Australia.
True ☑ **False** ☐ **Not given** ☐

1 He gets up at 7:30am.
True ☐ **False** ☐ **Not given** ☐

2 He doesn't work in an office.
True ☐ **False** ☐ **Not given** ☐

3 He likes his job.
True ☐ **False** ☐ **Not given** ☐

4 He has lunch with his friends.
True ☐ **False** ☐ **Not given** ☐

5 He has a dog.
True ☐ **False** ☐ **Not given** ☐

6 He goes swimming most weekends.
True ☐ **False** ☐ **Not given** ☐

MY DAY

HOME | ENTRIES | ABOUT | CONTACT

MY ROUTINE

Hi, my name's Edward. I live in Sydney, Australia. I get up at 7am every morning. I have breakfast at 7:30am and I take the bus to work. I start work at 9am every day. I don't work in an office. I'm a gardener and I work outside. I have lunch with my friends Steve and Vicky at 1pm. I leave work at 5:30pm. After work, I go swimming or I play tennis. In the evening I walk in the park with my dog. I go to bed at 10:30pm. Most weekends, I meet friends and I like watching movies. I like Sydney. It's a great city.

2.6 CONECTA EL INICIO Y EL FINAL DE CADA FRASE

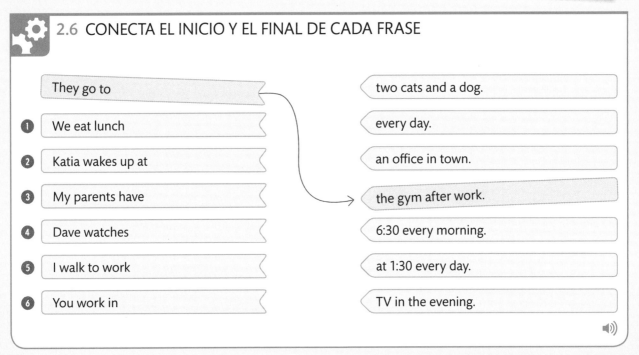

They go to	two cats and a dog.
1 We eat lunch	every day.
2 Katia wakes up at	an office in town.
3 My parents have	the gym after work.
4 Dave watches	6:30 every morning.
5 I walk to work	at 1:30 every day.
6 You work in	TV in the evening.

2.7 ESCRIBE CADA FRASE DE DOS MANERAS DISTINTAS

She lives in Britain.	She does not live in Britain.	She doesn't live in Britain.
① I work in a school.		
②	Sam does not eat lunch at 1pm.	
③		We don't leave home at 7:45am.
④ They like pizza.		
⑤	Sia does not watch TV every day.	
⑥		My friend doesn't have a dog.
⑦ You get up early.		
⑧	I do not have a new coat.	
⑨		He doesn't finish work at 5:30pm.

2.8 UTILIZA EL DIAGRAMA PARA CREAR 15 FRASES CORRECTAS Y DILAS EN VOZ ALTA

Lucy doesn't walk to work.

Lucy		walk	to work.
I	doesn't	get up	early.
They	don't	eat	breakfast.

Do you like cats?

Do you	like	cats?
Does John	work	soccer?
		in an office?

03 Hoy llevo...

Puedes utilizar el present continuous para hablar de lo que está ocurriendo ahora. Se suele utilizar para describir la ropa que la gente lleva puesta, lo que está utilizando o diciendo.

Lenguaje El present continuous

Aa Vocabulario Ropa y actividades

Habilidad Hablar sobre lo que está ocurriendo

3.1 TACHA LA PALABRA INCORRECTA DE CADA FRASE

Sandra is / ~~are~~ having her dinner.

❶ Glen is / are cleaning his car.

❷ April is / are watching a film.

❸ Peter and Frank is / are wearing suits.

❹ James is / are painting the kitchen.

❺ We is / are traveling around China.

❻ You is / are listening to an interesting song.

❼ Doug is / are reading a newspaper.

3.2 ESCUCHA EL AUDIO Y NUMERA LAS IMÁGENES EN EL ORDEN EN QUE SE DESCRIBEN

18

3.3 COMPLETA LOS ESPACIOS PONIENDO LOS VERBOS EN PRESENT CONTINUOUS

Mario _is walking_ (walk) his dog in the park.

❶ Anne _____ (wait) for her brother.

❷ Pedro _____ (cook) pizza for dinner.

❸ Mike _____ (mow) the lawn.

❹ Cynthia _____ (lie) on the sofa.

❺ Jane _____ (go) to the theater.

❻ I _____ (work) at the moment.

❼ Colin _____ (listen) to some music.

❽ Our children _____ (play) in a band.

❾ We _____ (drink) lemonade.

❿ Stefan _____ (come) to our party.

⓫ They _____ (eat) pasta for dinner.

⓬ Roberta _____ (wear) a sweater.

⓭ You _____ (play) tennis with John.

3.4 CONECTA EL INICIO Y EL FINAL DE CADA FRASE

Julie doesn't usually wear dresses,

❶ Paula doesn't often watch TV,

❷ Sven usually cooks at home,

❸ I often go to bed at 11pm,

❹ Janet is working at home today,

❺ Ravi usually wears casual clothes,

❻ Tim usually has cereal for breakfast,

❼ We usually go on vacation to Greece,

❽ I almost always drive to work,

❾ Nelson is drinking wine today,

❿ You usually wear pants,

but tonight she's watching a good movie.

but this evening I'm going to bed early.

but today he's eating at a restaurant.

but today she's wearing a bright red dress.

but today you're wearing a skirt.

but he normally drinks beer.

but today I'm walking as my car won't start.

but this morning he's having eggs.

but this year we're visiting Italy.

but today he's wearing a business suit.

but she usually works in an office.

3.5 TACHA LA PALABRA INCORRECTA DE CADA FRASE

They isn't / aren't wearing coats.

1 Vlad isn't / aren't playing soccer.

2 We isn't / aren't working today.

3 Manek isn't / aren't wearing a tie.

4 We isn't / aren't coming to the party.

5 Clarice isn't / aren't having dinner today.

6 Jonathan isn't / aren't walking the dog.

7 Mark and Trevor isn't / aren't going to the theater.

8 Pedro isn't / aren't wearing a suit.

9 Sally and Clive isn't / aren't going on vacation.

10 Sebastian isn't / aren't watching the movie.

11 You isn't / aren't working hard enough.

3.6 ESCRIBE LAS FRASES EN SU OTRA FORMA

Karl is writing.	Karl isn't writing.
1 Angelica is watching TV.	
2	I'm not working at home.
3 We're playing soccer.	
4	Ginny isn't eating a burger.
5 Sharon is listening to music.	
6	They aren't drinking soda.
7 We're going shopping.	
8	Anita isn't visiting Athens.
9 Pete's playing tennis.	
10	You aren't speaking Dutch.
11 Paul's wearing a hat.	
12	I am not walking home.
13 Steven is going swimming.	

3.7 VUELVE A ESCRIBIR LAS FRASES PONIENDO LAS PALABRAS EN SU ORDEN CORRECTO

| wearing | Greg | isn't | a | suit. |

Greg isn't wearing a suit.

5 | cooking | Trevor | dinner. | his | is |

_____

1 | on | going | this | vacation | year. | Kate | isn't |

_____

6 | traveling | Mr. Smith | is | Singapore. | to |

_____

2 | walk. | is | the | dog | Tracy | for | a | taking |

_____

7 | today. | playing | aren't | soccer | They |

_____

3 | isn't | Irena | to | party. | coming | the |

_____

8 | a | am | pair | of | shoes. | I | buying | new |

_____

4 | walking | We | to | today. | school | are |

_____

9 | aren't | coat | a | You | today. | wearing |

_____

🔊

3.8 MARCA LAS FRASES QUE CORRESPONDEN A LOS DIBUJOS

Deborah is wearing a hat. ☑
Deborah isn't wearing a hat. ☐

5 Sal is wearing a short coat. ☐
Sal is wearing a long coat. ☐

1 Jenny is wearing a red dress. ☐
Jenny is wearing pants. ☐

6 Mo is reading a book. ☐
Mo is watching a movie. ☐

2 Gemma is driving to work. ☐
Gemma isn't driving to work. ☐

7 Emily is wearing glasses. ☐
Emily is wearing a scarf. ☐

3 We are dancing. ☐
We are singing. ☐

8 Jo is speaking on her cellphone. ☐
Jo is listening to music. ☐

4 Brendan is eating a burger. ☐
Brendan isn't eating a burger. ☐

9 Kate is wearing jeans. ☐
Kate is wearing a skirt. ☐

🔊

04 ¿Qué está pasando?

Puedes utilizar el present continuous para hacer preguntas sobre algo que está ocurriendo ahora, en el momento en que se habla.

⚙ **Lenguaje** Preguntas con el present continuous
Aa Vocabulario Actividades y aparatos electrónicos
🧩 **Habilidad** Preguntar sobre el presente

4.1 RELACIONA CADA PREGUNTA CON SU RESPUESTA

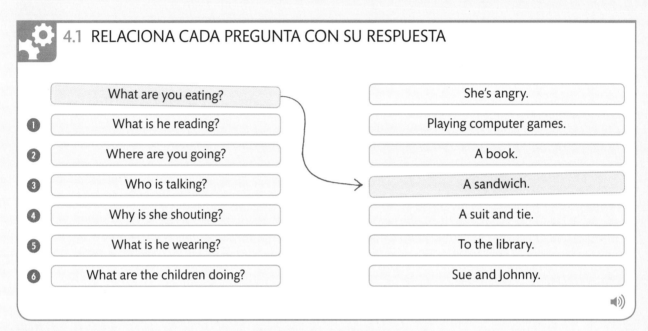

What are you eating?	She's angry.
❶ What is he reading?	Playing computer games.
❷ Where are you going?	A book.
❸ Who is talking?	A sandwich.
❹ Why is she shouting?	A suit and tie.
❺ What is he wearing?	To the library.
❻ What are the children doing?	Sue and Johnny.

4.2 COMPLETA LOS ESPACIOS CON LAS PALABRAS DEL RECUADRO

Jack is ___carrying___ a briefcase.

❹ Jane is _____ the dog.

❶ Lenny is _____ a tie today.

❺ Simon is _____ to music.

❷ Sarah is _____ dinner.

❻ Pat is _____ to work.

❸ Frank is _____ in the park.

❼ Gavin is _____ breakfast.

| carrying | listening | walking | eating | wearing | driving | running | cooking |

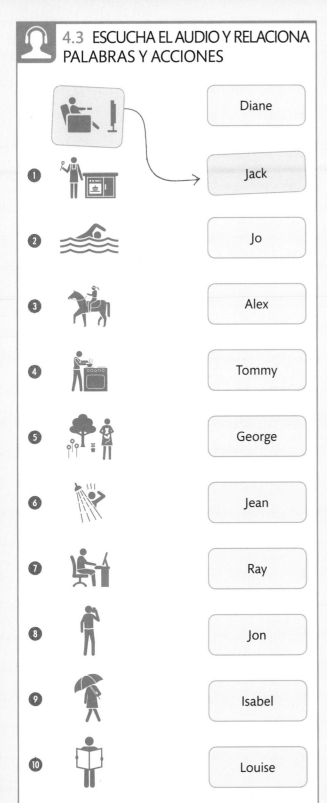

4.3 ESCUCHA EL AUDIO Y RELACIONA PALABRAS Y ACCIONES

Diane

1 Jack

2 Jo

3 Alex

4 Tommy

5 George

6 Jean

7 Ray

8 Jon

9 Isabel

10 Louise

4.4 VUELVE A ESCRIBIR LAS FRASES CORRIGIENDO LOS ERRORES

Jack and Mike is watching a film
Jack and Mike are watching a film.

1 I are doing my English homework.

_____

2 He is make breakfast.

_____

3 She are reading a magazine.

_____

4 They is running by the river.

_____

5 I is writing an email.

_____

6 We are listen to music.

_____

7 She am driving to London.

_____

8 He are taking a bath.

_____

9 They are do the shopping.

_____

10 I are eating a pizza.

_____

11 You is riding a motorcycle.

_____

12 We am going to bed.

_____

4.5 VUELVE A ESCRIBIR LAS FRASES COMO PREGUNTAS QUE COMIENCEN CON "WHAT"

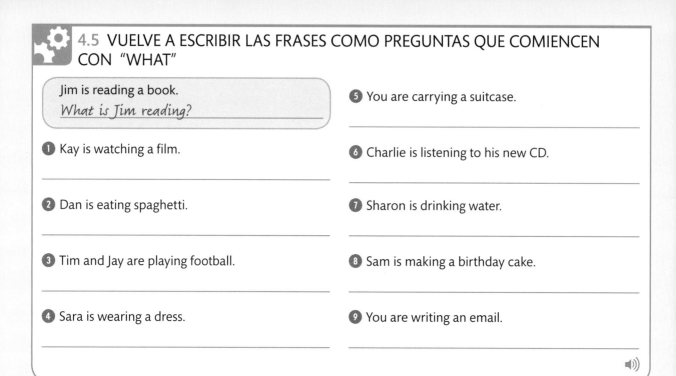

Jim is reading a book.
What is Jim reading?

❶ Kay is watching a film.

❷ Dan is eating spaghetti.

❸ Tim and Jay are playing football.

❹ Sara is wearing a dress.

❺ You are carrying a suitcase.

❻ Charlie is listening to his new CD.

❼ Sharon is drinking water.

❽ Sam is making a birthday cake.

❾ You are writing an email.

4.6 VUELVE A ESCRIBIR LAS FRASES PONIENDO LAS PALABRAS EN SU ORDEN CORRECTO

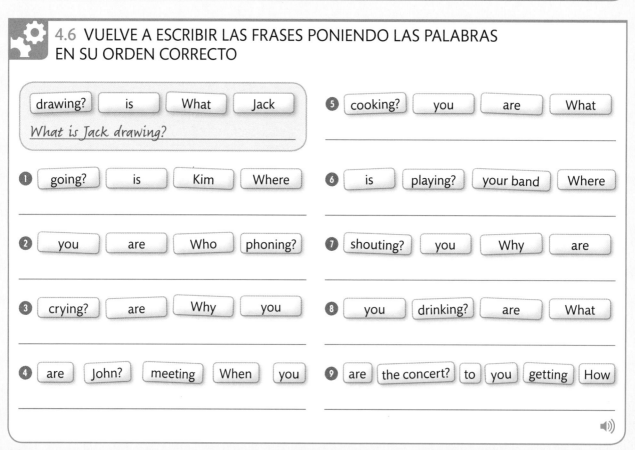

drawing? | is | What | Jack
What is Jack drawing?

❶ going? | is | Kim | Where

❷ you | are | Who | phoning?

❸ crying? | are | Why | you

❹ are | John? | meeting | When | you

❺ cooking? | you | are | What

❻ is | playing? | your band | Where

❼ shouting? | you | Why | are

❽ you | drinking? | are | What

❾ are | the concert? | to | you | getting | How

4.7 ESCUCHA EL AUDIO Y RELACIONA LOS REGALOS CON LAS PERSONAS

❶ ❷ ❸ ❹ ❺

Robert | Betty | Peter's mom | Dan | Claude | Pedro

4.8 OBSERVA LOS DIBUJOS Y RESPONDE AL AUDIO EN VOZ ALTA

What is Louise wearing?

Louise is wearing a red dress.

❶ What are they drinking?

_____ some coffee.

❷ What is Meg eating?

_____ a pizza.

❸ What is Louise riding?

_____ a horse.

❹ What is Paul using?

_____ his computer.

❺ What is Philippa baking?

_____ a cake.

05 Tipos de verbos

Puedes utilizar la mayoría de verbos en su forma continua para describir acciones en curso. Algunos verbos no pueden utilizarse así. Son los llamados verbos de estado.

⚙ **Lenguaje** Verbos de acción y de estado

Aa Vocabulario Actividades

🧩 **Habilidad** Utilizar verbos de estado

5.1 ESCRIBE LAS PALABRAS DEL RECUADRO EN SU GRUPO CORRECTO

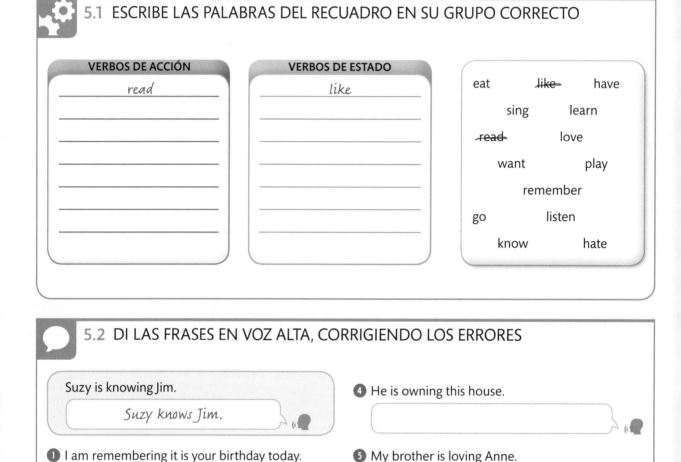

VERBOS DE ACCIÓN

read

VERBOS DE ESTADO

like

eat ~~like~~ have

sing learn

~~read~~ love

want play

remember

go listen

know hate

5.2 DI LAS FRASES EN VOZ ALTA, CORRIGIENDO LOS ERRORES

Suzy is knowing Jim.

Suzy knows Jim.

1 I am remembering it is your birthday today.

2 Dan is wanting a drink.

3 You are having two sisters.

4 He is owning this house.

5 My brother is loving Anne.

6 We are owning a horse.

7 My dad is hating pizza.

5.3 TACHA LAS PALABRAS INCORRECTAS DE CADA FRASE

 I want / ~~am wanting~~ some juice please.

① Greg plays / is playing tennis now.

② Mo watches / is watching TV right now.

③ We have / are having a new dog.

④ You don't like / aren't liking snakes.

⑤ Dom goes / is going to school now. 🔊

5.4 ESCUCHA EL AUDIO Y COMPLETA LOS ESPACIOS

Jane habla con su familia sobre su vida en Los Ángeles.

Jane ___*lives*___ in Los Angeles.

① Jane _____ at the school near her apartment.

② Jane really _____ teaching.

③ Jane _____ to restaurants on the weekend.

④ Jane _____ three children.

⑤ Ben _____ soccer with his friends.

⑥ Silvia _____ a film at the movie theater.

⑦ Mike _____ to music in his room.

Aa 5.5 RELACIONA LAS IMÁGENES CON LAS FRASES CORRECTAS

①

②

③

④

| She hates snakes. | He's watching TV. | Samantha has three children. | She's listening to music. | They're running to school. |

🔊

Aa **6.1 SENTIMIENTOS Y ÁNIMOS** ESCRIBE LAS PALABRAS DEL RECUADRO BAJO SU IMAGEN

_____ happy _____

① _____

② _____

③ _____

⑥ _____

⑦ _____

⑧ _____

⑨ _____

⑫ _____

⑬ _____

⑭ _____

⑮ _____

⑱ _____

⑲ _____

⑳ _____

㉑ _____

④ _____

⑤ _____

⑩ _____

⑪ _____

⑯ _____

⑰ _____

㉒ _____

㉓ _____

relaxed   angry

disappointed   ~~happy~~

irritated   proud

scared   calm

surprised   distracted

confused   lonely

unhappy   excited

grateful   stressed

tired   anxious

bored   worried

jealous   confident

curious   amused

🔊

29

07 Cómo te sientes

Una parte importante de nuestras conversaciones diarias se basa en hablar de nuestros sentimientos. Utiliza el present continuous para hablar de cómo te sientes.

⚙ **Lenguaje** "Feeling" y emociones
Aa Vocabulario Adjetivos de emociones
🧩 **Habilidad** Hablar de cómo te sientes

Aa 7.1 BUSCA EN LA TABLA 10 ADJETIVOS DE EMOCIÓN

```
N S A B L I N E R V O U S L X N G O Q H N V
R D E M O S M D S C A L M R S M D T M A R D
S I N T E R P I U T C U D E R A I I T P U I
E K A T E B E A R X I N P E B A D R S P N G
M E X C I T E D F L A N G R Y A K E I Y N C
P T L S L C A Z I O R P L E A S E D L R I O
```

~~excited~~   nervous   bored   pleased   bad   calm   happy   sad   angry   tired

---

⚙ 7.2 TACHA LA PALABRA INCORRECTA DE CADA FRASE

We are feeling ~~confident~~ / nervous.

 ❹ Samantha is feeling happy / sad.

 ❶ Alexander is feeling excited / calm.

 ❺ I'm feeling miserable / happy.

 ❷ Danny is feeling tired / cheerful.

 ❻ Christopher is feeling sad / curious.

 ❸ Peter is feeling anxious / proud.

 ❼ Waldo is feeling happy / bored.

🔊

7.3 RELACIONA LOS DIBUJOS CON LAS FRASES CORRECTAS

Claire is feeling happy because it's her birthday.

① Jack is feeling sad because it is raining.

② Shaun is feeling excited because he's watching soccer.

③ Chris is feeling tired because it's very late.

④ Angelo is feeling bored because his book isn't interesting.

⑤ Marge is feeling annoyed because Jack is being naughty.

⑥ Carl is feeling sad because he misses his dog.

⑦ Jimmy is feeling pleased because he has a new car.

⑧ Rachel is feeling nervous because she has an exam.

⑨ Ron is feeling relaxed because he is on vacation.

⑩ Sandy is feeling jealous because her sister has a new toy.

⑪ Anne is feeling angry because her boyfriend is late.

7.4 UTILIZA EL DIAGRAMA PARA CREAR 12 FRASES CORRECTAS Y DILAS EN VOZ ALTA

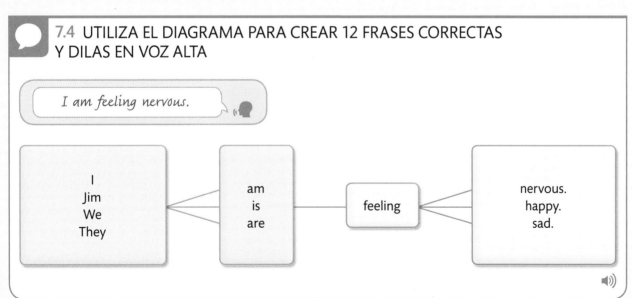

I am feeling nervous.

| I / Jim / We / They | am / is / are | feeling | nervous. / happy. / sad. |

7.5 ESCUCHA EL AUDIO Y RESPONDE A LAS PREGUNTAS

Varias personas cuentan a sus amigos cómo se sienten hoy.

Tammy is feeling...
nervous. ☐ happy. ☑ amused. ☐

❶ Charles is feeling...
scared. ☐ bored. ☐ angry. ☐

❷ Colin is feeling...
tired. ☐ sad. ☐ happy. ☐

❸ Jim is feeling...
nervous. ☐ sad. ☐ angry. ☐

❹ Greg is feeling...
tired. ☐ sad. ☐ annoyed. ☐

❺ Tanya is feeling...
irritated. ☐ tired. ☐ nervous. ☐

❻ Bill and Susan are feeling...
excited. ☐ scared. ☐ nervous. ☐

❼ Giles is feeling...
happy. ☐ nervous. ☐ furious. ☐

❽ Arnold is feeling...
tired. ☐ angry. ☐ relaxed. ☐

❾ Katy is feeling...
tired. ☐ bored. ☐ angry. ☐

7.6 CONECTA LAS PAREJAS DE FRASES RELACIONADAS

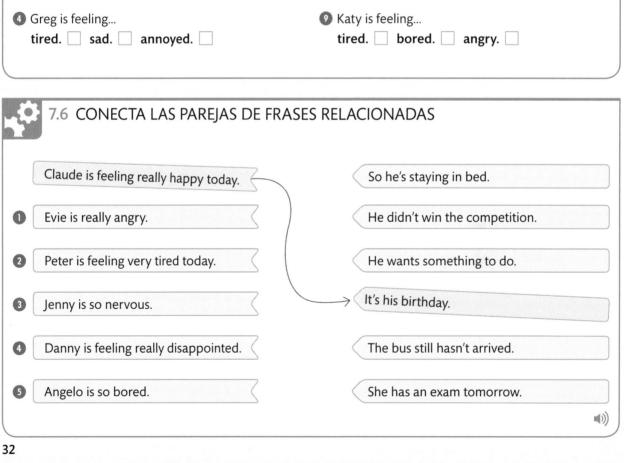

Claude is feeling really happy today.

❶ Evie is really angry.

❷ Peter is feeling very tired today.

❸ Jenny is so nervous.

❹ Danny is feeling really disappointed.

❺ Angelo is so bored.

So he's staying in bed.

He didn't win the competition.

He wants something to do.

It's his birthday.

The bus still hasn't arrived.

She has an exam tomorrow.

Aa 7.7 COMPLETA LOS ESPACIOS CON LAS PALABRAS DEL RECUADRO

I have my exam tomorrow. It's science, and I'm not very good at it. I'm so ____nervous____ .

3 I don't know what to do. There's nothing on TV. I'm really _____ .

1 It's my birthday tomorrow. I really can't wait! I'm so _____ .

4 This book is really depressing. So many bad things happen. I'm feeling really _____ .

2 I don't like this house. It's so dark. Is that a spider? I'm feeling very _____ .

5 My girlfriend's forgotten my birthday. And she forgot last year. I'm so _____ .

| angry | ~~nervous~~ | scared | sad | excited | bored |

Aa 8.1 **TRANSPORTE** ESCRIBE LAS PALABRAS DEL RECUADRO DEBAJO DE SUS DIBUJOS

bicycle

1 _____

2 _____

3 _____

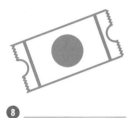

8 _____

9 _____

10 _____

11 _____

16 _____

17 _____

18 _____

19 _____

20 _____

21 _____

22 _____

23 _____

4 _____

5 _____

6 _____

7 _____

12 _____

13 _____

14 _____

15 _____

taxi	steering wheel	walk	taxi rank
plane	ticket	bus stop	ride a bike
road	car	train	fly a plane
boat	yacht	port	tram
~~bicycle~~	bus	helicopter	fare
airport	drive a car	ship	train station

09 Rutinas y excepciones

Utiliza el present simple para describir rutinas, y el present continuous para explicar lo haces en este momento. Estos dos tiempos verbales a menudo pueden utilizarse conjuntamente.

⚙ **Lenguaje** Excepciones
Aa Vocabulario Marcas de tiempo
✦ **Habilidad** Contraponer rutinas y excepciones

9.1 COMPLETA LOS ESPACIOS PONIENDO LOS VERBOS EN LOS TIEMPOS CORRECTOS

Doug usually ___*orders*___ (order) a pizza on Fridays, but today he ___*is cooking*___ (cook).

1. Tony often _____ (go) for a swim in the evening, but today he _____ (visit) a friend.

2. Today Baz _____ (have) eggs, but he mostly _____ (eat) cereal for breakfast.

3. John's sister usually _____ (drive) to work, but today she _____ (walk).

4. Clara usually _____ (sleep) in the afternoon, but today she _____ (go) for a walk.

5. My cousins often _____ (play) soccer together, but today they _____ (play) golf.

6. He normally _____ (go) on vacation to Peru, but this year he _____ (visit) Greece.

7. Jenny usually _____ (watch) TV in the evening, but tonight she _____ (read).

8. Abe often _____ (play) soccer on Fridays, but today he _____ (watch) a game.

9. Tonight our dog _____ (sleep) in the kitchen, but he often _____ (sleep) outside.

10. Liza usually _____ (go) to the gym after work, but today she _____ (rest).

11. They often _____ (go) running on Saturdays, but today they _____ (shop).

9.2 VUELVE A ESCRIBIR LAS FRASES CORRIGIENDO LOS ERRORES

> Sam usually is playing tennis on Thursdays, but today he play golf with his brother.
> *Sam usually plays tennis on Thursdays, but today he is playing golf with his brother.*

❶ My wife usually worked until 5pm, but this evening she working until 7:30pm.

_____

❷ Jim often is listening to the radio in the evening, but tonight he go to a party.

_____

❸ I often meeting my friends in the evening, but tonight I meets my grandmother.

_____

❹ Mrs. Brown teaches English this week, but she normally was teaching geography.

_____

❺ Hank walk in the Pyrenees this week, but he usually going to work every day.

_____

9.3 DI LAS FRASES EN VOZ ALTA, PONIENDO LOS VERBOS EN LOS TIEMPOS CORRECTOS

> Mike _____*is wearing*_____ (wear) a T-shirt today, but he normally _____*wears*_____ (wear) a suit.

❶ I normally _____ (go) to bed at 11pm, but tonight I _____ (meet) some friends.

❷ Today Jane _____ (eat) a sandwich, but she often _____ (have) soup for lunch.

❸ Sam usually _____ (drink) coffee, but this morning he _____ (drink) tea.

❹ Tonight we _____ (have) water with our dinner, but we usually _____ (have) juice.

❺ I usually _____ (feel) confident about exams, but today I _____ (feel) nervous.

37

10 Vocabulario

Aa **10.1 EL CUERPO** ESCRIBE LAS PALABRAS DEL RECUADRO BAJO SU IMAGEN

mouth

1 _____

2 _____

3 _____

4 _____

8 _____

9 _____

10 _____

11 _____

12 _____

16 _____

17 _____

18 _____

19 _____

20 _____

24 _____

25 _____

26 _____

27 _____

28 _____

5 _____

6 _____

7 _____

lips	chest
eye	nose	arm
eyebrow	head
ankle	toes
cheek	shoulders	shin
neck	foot
stomach	fingers
fingernail	thumb
hair	chin	leg
eyelashes	tooth
heel	face	teeth
knee	hand
knuckles	~~mouth~~
thigh	ear

13 _____

14 _____

15 _____

21 _____

22 _____

23 _____

29 _____

30 _____

31 _____

11 ¿Qué te ocurre?

Hay muchas maneras de decir que te encuentras mal. En general usarás la expresión negativa "not well" para hablar de dolencias generales, y "hurts", "ache" o "pain" para dolores específicos.

⚙ **Lenguaje** Quejarse de la salud
Aa Vocabulario Partes del cuerpo y dolor
Habilidad Decir lo que te ocurre

 11.1 VUELVE A ESCRIBIR LAS FRASES CORRIGIENDO LOS ERRORES

> Doug is not **feel** very well today, so he is not coming to work.
> _Doug is not feeling very well today, so he is not coming to work._

❶ I **don't** feeling well today. I'm sorry. Let's meet next week instead.

_____

❷ May and Clara are **feel** sick today. They're going to stay at home.

_____

❸ Cathy **not** feeling well. She is not going swimming today.

_____

❹ Jerry is **feel** really sick, but he's still going to work.

_____

❺ We don't **feeling** well, so we aren't coming to the party tonight.

_____

❻ Alexander **not** feel well. He's going to stay at home today.

_____

❼ They don't **feeling** well. They're not going to visit their uncle and aunt today.

_____

❽ Hilary isn't **feels** well. She can't come to the movies tonight.

_____

❾ Lee **feel** sick. He can't come to the sales meeting today.

_____

❿ John and Diana is not feeling well. They are going to leave work early today.

_____

◀))

11.2 COMPLETA LOS ESPACIOS CON LAS PALABRAS DEL RECUADRO

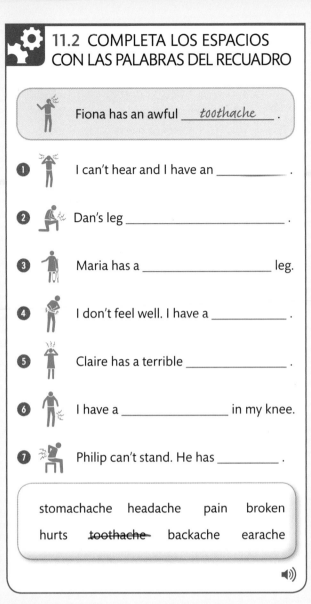

Fiona has an awful ___toothache___ .

❶ I can't hear and I have an _____ .

❷ Dan's leg _____ .

❸ Maria has a _____ leg.

❹ I don't feel well. I have a _____ .

❺ Claire has a terrible _____ .

❻ I have a _____ in my knee.

❼ Philip can't stand. He has _____ .

stomachache   headache   pain   broken

hurts   ~~toothache~~   backache   earache

11.3 ESCUCHA EL AUDIO Y RESPONDE A LAS PREGUNTAS

Alfred va a ver al Dr. McCloud y le cuenta sus problemas de salud.

Alfred's back is hurting.
True ✓ **False** ☐ **Not given** ☐

❶ Alfred's legs hurt.
True ☐ **False** ☐ **Not given** ☐

❷ His arm is hurting.
True ☐ **False** ☐ **Not given** ☐

❸ Alfred's arm is broken.
True ☐ **False** ☐ **Not given** ☐

❹ He has a pain in his shoulder.
True ☐ **False** ☐ **Not given** ☐

❺ Alfred has a pain in his foot.
True ☐ **False** ☐ **Not given** ☐

❻ Alfred has a toothache.
True ☐ **False** ☐ **Not given** ☐

❼ He has a headache.
True ☐ **False** ☐ **Not given** ☐

11.4 UTILIZA EL DIAGRAMA PARA CREAR 12 FRASES CORRECTAS Y DILAS EN VOZ ALTA

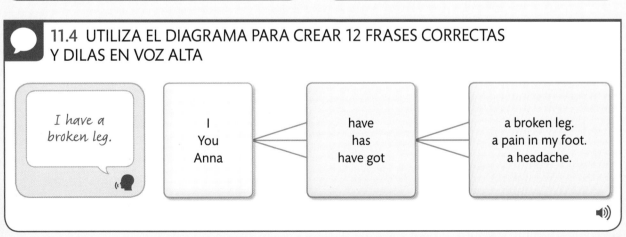

I have a broken leg.

| I You Anna | have has have got | a broken leg. a pain in my foot. a headache. |

12 Vocabulario

Aa 12.1 **EL TIEMPO** ESCRIBE LAS PALABRAS DEL RECUADRO BAJO SU IMAGEN

warm

1 _____

2 _____

3 _____

8 _____

9 _____

10 _____

11 _____

16 _____

17 _____

18 _____

19 _____

20 _____

21 _____

22 _____

23 _____

4 _____

5 _____

6 _____

7 _____

12 _____

13 _____

14 _____

15 _____

cloud	hot	snow	flood
freezing	humidity	cold	rainbow
blue sky	hail	thunder	puddle
wet	tornado	boiling	gale
~~warm~~	lightning	wind	ice
rain	sun	temperature	dry

🔊

43

13 ¿Qué tiempo hace?

Existen muchas maneras diferentes de hablar del tiempo. Utiliza el verbo "to be" con palabras y frases relacionadas con el tiempo para hablar de la temperatura y del clima.

⚙ **Lenguaje** Descripción del tiempo
Aa Vocabulario Palabras sobre la temperatura
Habilidad Hablar del tiempo

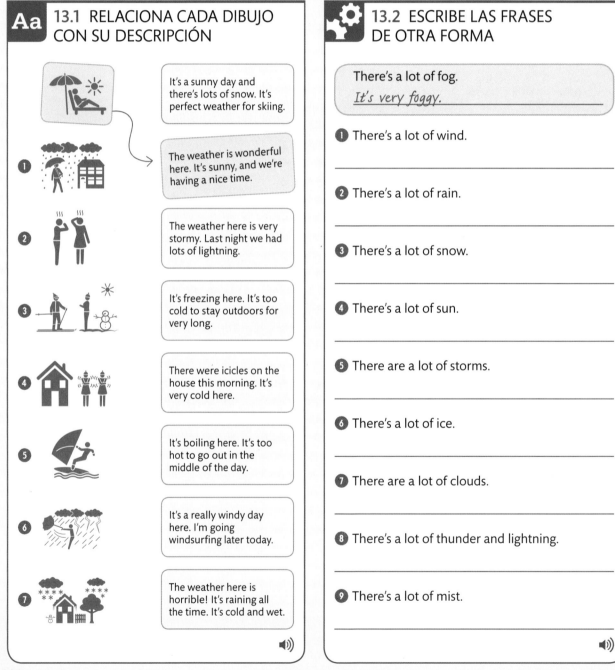

Aa 13.1 RELACIONA CADA DIBUJO CON SU DESCRIPCIÓN

It's a sunny day and there's lots of snow. It's perfect weather for skiing.

The weather is wonderful here. It's sunny, and we're having a nice time.

1

The weather here is very stormy. Last night we had lots of lightning.

2

It's freezing here. It's too cold to stay outdoors for very long.

3

There were icicles on the house this morning. It's very cold here.

4

It's boiling here. It's too hot to go out in the middle of the day.

5

It's a really windy day here. I'm going windsurfing later today.

6

The weather here is horrible! It's raining all the time. It's cold and wet.

7

⚙ 13.2 ESCRIBE LAS FRASES DE OTRA FORMA

There's a lot of fog.
It's very foggy.

❶ There's a lot of wind.

_____

❷ There's a lot of rain.

_____

❸ There's a lot of snow.

_____

❹ There's a lot of sun.

_____

❺ There are a lot of storms.

_____

❻ There's a lot of ice.

_____

❼ There are a lot of clouds.

_____

❽ There's a lot of thunder and lightning.

_____

❾ There's a lot of mist.

_____

13.3 COMPLETA LOS ESPACIOS CON LAS PALABRAS DEL RECUADRO

It's ___*boiling*___ here in Morocco. It's 104°F.

❹ It's 14°F here and it's snowy. It's _____ .

❶ Be careful. There's _____ on the road.

❺ Oh no, it's _____ . We can't play tennis now.

❷ The weather's beautiful. It's hot and _____ .

❻ It's very _____ . The airport is closed.

❸ It's quite _____ here. The temperature is 68°F.

❼ There's a _____ . We can't play golf.

| warm | freezing | ice | foggy | ~~boiling~~ | raining | storm | sunny |

13.4 ESCUCHA EL AUDIO Y RESPONDE A LAS PREGUNTAS

Un locutor de radio habla sobre el tiempo que hace en Europa.

Where is it sunny?
Northern Europe ☐ **Central Europe** ☑

❸ Which is the hottest city in Europe?
Madrid ☐ **Rome** ☐ **Lisbon** ☐

❶ Where is it not raining?
Britain ☐ **Spain** ☐ **Germany** ☐

❹ Where should you not drive?
Italy ☐ **Finland** ☐ **Sweden** ☐

❷ Which is the coldest city in Europe?
London ☐ **Copenhagen** ☐ **Berlin** ☐

❺ Where will there be no clouds?
Britain ☐ **Scandinavia** ☐ **France** ☐

13.5 UTILIZA EL DIAGRAMA PARA CREAR 10 FRASES CORRECTAS Y DILAS EN VOZ ALTA

There's a lot of rain at the moment.

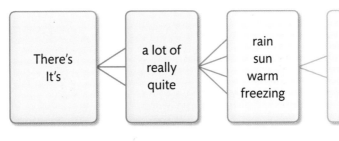

There's
It's

a lot of
really
quite

rain
sun
warm
freezing

at the moment.
in London today.

14 Vocabulario

Aa 14.1 **VIAJAR** ESCRIBE LAS PALABRAS DEL RECUADRO BAJO SU IMAGEN

stay in a hotel

1 _____

2 _____

3 _____

6 _____

7 _____

8 _____

9 _____

12 _____

13 _____

14 _____

15 _____

18 _____

19 _____

20 _____

21 _____

4 _____

5 _____

10 _____

11 _____

16 _____

17 _____

22 _____

23 _____

leave a hotel   luggage

security   road trip

hand luggage   runway

on time   passport control

miss a flight   board a plane

~~stay in a hotel~~   reception

apartment   pack your bags

late   arrive at the airport

boarding card   hostel

arrive at a hotel   get on a bus

fly in a plane   go sightseeing

get off a bus   cruise

15 Hacer comparaciones

Los adjetivos comparativos sirven para indicar las diferencias entre dos palabras. Utilízalos antes de la palabra "than" para comparar personas, lugares o cosas.

 Lenguaje Adjetivos comparativos
Aa Vocabulario Viajes y países
Habilidad Comparar cosas

15.1 COMPLETA LOS ESPACIOS CON LAS PALABRAS DEL RECUADRO

The bag is bigger than the _watch_ .

1 I'm _____ than you are.

2 A train is _____ than a bus.

3 79°F is _____ than 64°F.

4 A car is faster than a _____ .

5 _____ is smaller than Russia.

6 Everest is higher than _____ .

7 6am is _____ than 9am.

8 A tiger is _____ than a pig.

9 Your dress is _____ than mine.

10 95°F is _____ than 110°F.

11 The Sahara is _____ than the Arctic.

12 11pm is _____ than 3pm.

13 An _____ is bigger than a mouse.

14 A plane is _____ than a car.

15 _____ is colder than milk.

16 Mars is _____ to Earth than Pluto.

17 Athens is _____ than Los Angeles.

France	later	taller	bigger	ice cream	bike
hotter	~~watch~~	colder	Mont Blanc	older	faster
prettier	hotter	earlier	faster	elephant	closer

Aa 15.2 BUSCA EN LA TABLA OCHO ADJETIVOS COMPARATIVOS Y ESCRÍBELOS EN SU LUGAR

```
V D I H O T T E R I T V
I H R L L U W L O W E R
B E Q R X D I R T I E R
I C A O L A T E R H Z X
G L Z S Y F Y B I C D P
G G R Y I (T H I N N E R)
E Q Z T T E L A R G E R
R U V I B N R L V Q G R
```

1. thin = _thinner_
2. easy = _____
3. late = _____
4. dirty = _____
5. large = _____
6. big = _____
7. hot = _____
8. low = _____

15.3 COMPLETA LOS ESPACIOS PONIENDO LOS ADJETIVOS EN SU FORMA COMPARATIVA

Platinum is very **expensive**. It's _____ *more expensive than* _____ gold.

1. This painting is **beautiful**. It's _____ that one.

2. Russian is very **difficult**. It's _____ Italian.

3. Rome is very **old**. It's _____ my city.

4. Pizza is very **tasty**. It's _____ pasta.

5. China is very **large**. It's _____ Germany.

6. Oslo is very **cold**. It's _____ Paris.

7. Science is very **difficult**. It's _____ geography.

8. Monaco is very **expensive**. It's _____ Berlin.

9. Mountain climbing is **dangerous**. It's _____ hiking.

10. This book is very **interesting**. It's _____ yours.

11. Skiing is **exciting**. It's _____ jogging.

🔊

15.4 ESCUCHA EL AUDIO Y RESPONDE A LAS PREGUNTAS

Dave llama a la agencia de viajes para contratar sus vacaciones.

Sicily is more expensive than Greece.
True ✓ **False** ☐

❸ The beaches in Sicily are more beautiful.
True ☐ **False** ☐

❶ The resort in Greece is bigger.
True ☐ **False** ☐

❹ Dave thinks Greek food is tastier.
True ☐ **False** ☐

❷ The resort in Sicily is more interesting.
True ☐ **False** ☐

❺ Sicily is hotter than Greece.
True ☐ **False** ☐

15.5 COMPLETA LOS ESPACIOS PONIENDO LOS ADJETIVOS EN SU FORMA COMPARATIVA

Nine o'clock is ___*later than*___ (late) seven o'clock.

Seven o'clock is ___*earlier than*___ (early) nine o'clock.

❶ Flying is _____ (safe) driving.

Driving is _____ (dangerous) flying.

❷ My computer is _____ (old) my phone.

My phone is _____ (new) my computer.

❸ The suitcase is _____ (heavy) the bag.

The bag is _____ (light) the suitcase.

❹ This champagne is _____ (expensive) that wine.

This wine is _____ (cheap) that champagne.

❺ 118°F is _____ (hot) 90°F.

90°F is _____ (cold) than 118°F.

15.6 DI LAS FRASES EN VOZ ALTA, COMPLETANDO LOS ESPACIOS CON EXPRESIONES COMPARATIVAS

A horse _____*is bigger than*_____ (big) a dog.

❶ 11pm _____ (late) 10pm.

❷ Gold _____ (cheap) platinum.

❸ Athens _____ (old) Los Angeles.

❹ Chess _____ (difficult) poker.

❺ Tennis _____ (energetic) walking.

15.7 DI LAS FRASES EN VOZ ALTA, COMPLETANDO LOS ESPACIOS CON EXPRESIONES COMPARATIVAS

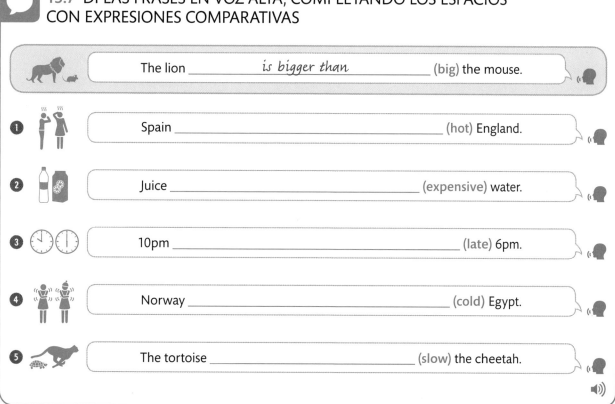

The lion _____*is bigger than*_____ (big) the mouse.

❶ Spain _____ (hot) England.

❷ Juice _____ (expensive) water.

❸ 10pm _____ (late) 6pm.

❹ Norway _____ (cold) Egypt.

❺ The tortoise _____ (slow) the cheetah.

16 Hablar sobre extremos

Utiliza adjetivos superlativos para hablar de extremos, como "the biggest" (el mayor) o "the smallest" (el más pequeño). Para adjetivos largos, forma el superlativo con "the most".

⚙ **Lenguaje** Adjetivos superlativos
Aa Vocabulario Animales, hechos y lugares
👣 **Habilidad** Hablar sobre extremos

16.1 COMPLETA LOS ESPACIOS ESCRIBIENDO LOS ADJETIVOS EN SU FORMA SUPERLATIVA

Death Valley in California is the _____*hottest*_____ (hot) place in the world.

1 The Great Wall of China is the _____ (long) wall in the world.

2 The African Bush Elephant is the _____ (big) land animal.

3 Vatican City is the _____ (small) country in the world.

4 The Burj Khalifa is the _____ (tall) building in the world.

5 The Amazon is the _____ (wide) river in the world.

6 Dolphins are in the top 10 _____ (intelligent) animals.

🔊

16.2 ESCRIBE LA FORMA SUPERLATIVA DE CADA ADJETIVO

high	*highest*		8	ugly	
1 small			9	clean	
2 big			10	dirty	
3 far			11	expensive	
4 high			12	new	
5 thin			13	old	
6 fat			14	intelligent	
7 beautiful			15	fast	

16.3 ESCUCHA EL AUDIO Y RESPONDE A LAS PREGUNTAS

Jane, Sue y Dan hablan de sus coches y sus teléfonos.

Who has the newest car?
Dan ☐   Jane ☐   Sue ☑

❶ Who has the fastest car?
Dan ☐   Jane ☐   Sue ☐

❷ Who has the biggest car?
Dan ☐   Jane ☐   Sue ☐

❸ Who has the most comfortable car?
Dan ☐   Jane ☐   Sue ☐

❹ Who has the newest phone?
Dan ☐   Jane ☐   Sue ☐

❺ Who is the safest driver?
Dan ☐   Jane ☐   Sue ☐

❻ Who drives the farthest?
Dan ☐   Jane ☐   Sue ☐

❼ Who is the most experienced driver?
Dan ☐   Jane ☐   Sue ☐

16.4 COMPLETA LOS ESPACIOS CON LA FORMA SUPERLATIVA DE LOS ADJETIVOS DEL RECUADRO

The tree is bigger than the car, but the house is the _____*biggest*_____.

❶ A rhino is heavier than a lion, but elephants are the _____ land animal.

❷ A whale is more intelligent than a shark, but dolphins are the _____ sea animal.

❸ The Regal is more expensive than the Grand, but the Plaza is the _____ hotel.

❹ The Statue of Liberty is taller than the Leaning Tower of Pisa, but Big Ben is the _____.

❺ The Thames is longer than the Trent, but the Severn is the _____ river in the UK.

| tall | intelligent | long | heavy | ~~big~~ | expensive |

16.5 ESCRIBE LA FORMA SUPERLATIVA DE ESTOS ADJETIVOS

| beautiful | = | *the most beautiful* |

1. expensive = _____
2. comfortable = _____
3. intelligent = _____
4. dangerous = _____
5. exciting = _____
6. impressive = _____
7. handsome = _____

🔊

16.6 LEE EL BLOG Y RESPONDE A LAS PREGUNTAS

Which is the most expensive hotel?
The Rialto ☐ **The Plaza** ☐ **The Grand** ☑

1. Which hotel is closest to the city center?
The Rialto ☐ **The Plaza** ☐ **The Grand** ☐

2. Which is the biggest hotel?
The Rialto ☐ **The Plaza** ☐ **The Grand** ☐

3. Which hotel provides the best breakfast?
The Rialto ☐ **The Plaza** ☐ **The Grand** ☐

4. Which is the most historic hotel?
The Rialto ☐ **The Plaza** ☐ **The Grand** ☐

5. Which is the newest hotel?
The Rialto ☐ **The Plaza** ☐ **The Grand** ☐

6. Which hotel has rooms with the most impressive views?
The Rialto ☐ **The Plaza** ☐ **The Grand** ☐

<> III 🔍 ⌂ C

Best Hotels

HOME | ENTRIES | ABOUT | CONTACT

THE TOP THREE

The Rialto
This hotel is perfect for a city break because it is right in the city center. It has 100 rooms and has been a hotel since 1925. Some rooms come with an impressive view of the castle. Rooms cost from $120 a night for a double, with a simple continental breakfast included.

The Plaza
This is a new hotel, with 80 rooms. The hotel attracts lots of business people as well as tourists. It is famed for having the best breakfast in the city. Rooms cost from $150 a night for a double.

The Grand
This is officially the oldest hotel in the city, so it has lots of history. With 120 rooms it is one of the biggest hotels in the city. Rooms cost from $180 a night for a double.

16.7 VUELVE A ESCRIBIR LAS FRASES CORRIGIENDO LOS ERRORES

> The older cave paintings in the world are about 40,000 years old.
> _The oldest cave paintings in the world are about 40,000 years old._

1 The Amazon rainforest has some of the more beautiful plants in the world.

_____

2 Mesopotamia is thought to be the home of the earlier civilization in the world.

_____

3 The British Museum is the more popular tourist attraction in the UK.

_____

4 New York City and Geneva are the more expensive cities in the world.

_____

5 Hippopotamuses are one of the world's more dangerous animals.

_____

16.8 DI LAS FRASES EN VOZ ALTA, COMPLETANDO LOS ESPACIOS CON SUPERLATIVOS

> Moscow is a very large city. It is _____ _the largest city_ _____ in Europe.

1 The Shanghai Tower is a very tall building. It is _____ in China.

2 The sloth is a very slow animal. It is _____ in the world.

3 The Vasco da Gama bridge in Portugal is very long. It is _____ in Europe.

4 The Dead Sea is a very low point on Earth. It is _____ on Earth.

5 Mount Elbrus in Russia is a very tall mountain. It is _____ in Europe.

17 Vocabulario

Aa **17.1 GEOGRAFÍA** ESCRIBE LAS PALABRAS DEL RECUADRO BAJO SU IMAGEN

sand dune

1 _____

2 _____

3 _____

8 _____

9 _____

10 _____

11 _____

16 _____

17 _____

18 _____

19 _____

ocean	rocks	coast	swamp
countryside	~~sand dune~~	river	polar region
volcano	iceberg	beach	waterfall

56

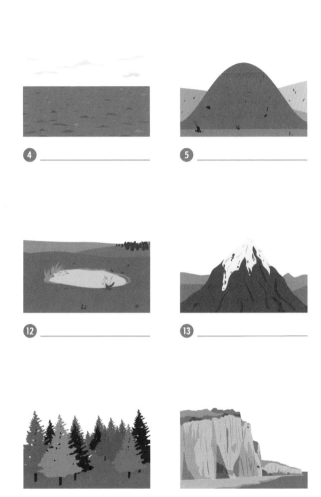

4 _____

5 _____

6 _____

7 _____

12 _____

13 _____

14 _____

15 _____

20 _____

21 _____

22 _____

23 _____

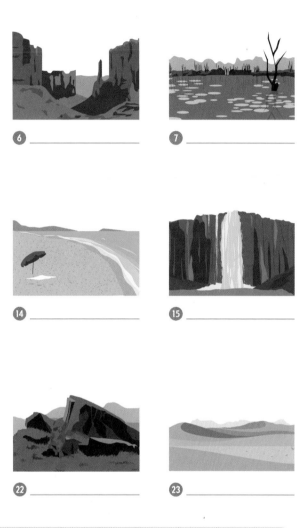

cave	woods	desert	oasis
valley	mountain	rainforest	canyon
pond	island	cliff	hill

18 Elecciones

"Which", "what", "and" y "or" son palabras útiles al hacer preguntas. Puedes utilizarlas para determinar si haces una pregunta en general o específica.

⚙ **Lenguaje** "Which" y "what"
Aa Vocabulario Palabras sobre geografía
Habilidad Hacer preguntas de múltiple respuesta

 18.1 TACHA LA PALABRA INCORRECTA DE CADA FRASE

🍔 + 🥤 Would you like a burger and / ~~or~~ soda for lunch?

❶ Would you like to stay in **and** / **or** watch a DVD tonight?

❷  Do you want to go to the Tower of London **and** / **or** the London Eye?

❸ Do you want pizza **and** / **or** salad for dinner tonight?

❹ Is Marianne a pop singer **and** / **or** a modern jazz singer?

❺ Can I pay for the washing machine in cash **and** / **or** by credit card?

❻ On birthdays, we open our presents **and** / **or** play party games.

❼ Do you want to go to a movie **and** / **or** the theater tomorrow night?

❽ Would you like to study French **and** / **or** German next year?

❾ Did you live in a house **and** / **or** an apartment when you were in Thailand?

❿ I had coffee **and** / **or** chocolate cake at the new café in town.

⓫   Would you like tea **and** / **or** coffee while you wait for your appointment?

🔊

18.2 MARCA LAS FRASES CORRECTAS

Which is the tallest building in Asia? ☐
What is the tallest building in Asia? ☑

① What is Tom's car, the red or the blue one? ☐
Which is Tom's car, the red or the blue one? ☐

② What is the biggest country in Europe? ☐
Which is the biggest country in Europe? ☐

③ What is bigger, a lion or a hippo? ☐
Which is bigger, a lion or a hippo? ☐

④ What would you like? Cake or cookies? ☐
Which would you like? Cake or cookies? ☐

⑤ What would you like to do this evening? ☐
Which would you like to do this evening? ☐

⑥ What shall we have for dinner tonight? ☐
Which shall we have for dinner tonight? ☐

⑦ What ink does he use, black or blue? ☐
Which ink does he use, black or blue? ☐

⑧ What is your favorite food? ☐
Which is your favorite food? ☐

⑨ What is the tallest mountain in the world? ☐
Which is the tallest mountain in the world? ☐

◀))

18.3 COMPLETA LOS ESPACIOS CON "WHICH" O "WHAT"

_____Which_____ would you like to visit, Peru, Chile, or Brazil?

① _____ would you like to do tomorrow when we meet?

② _____ is the fastest animal in the world?

③ _____ restaurant would you like to go to, the Italian or the Indian one?

④ _____ language does he speak, French, Italian, or Spanish?

⑤ _____ is your favorite subject at school?

⑥ _____ of these houses does Mike live in?

◀))

18.4 COMPLETA LOS ESPACIOS CON LA FORMA COMPARATIVA O SUPERLATIVA DE LOS ADJETIVOS

Anna is _____ better _____ (good) at skiing than I am.

① My exam results were _____ (bad) than Frank's.

② The Plaza is the _____ (good) hotel in the city.

③ My new workplace is _____ (far) from my house than my old one.

④ I am a _____ (good) driver than my brother.

⑤ Don't go to Gigi's. It's the _____ (bad) café in town.

⑥ Neptune is the _____ (far) planet from the Sun.

18.5 COMBINA LAS DOS FRASES PARA FORMAR UNA SOLA Y DILA EN VOZ ALTA

I am good at tennis. My sister is better.

My sister _____ is better at _____ tennis than I am.

① I am bad at soccer. My brother is worse.

My brother is _____

② The red T-shirt is $10. The blue T-shirt is $15.

The blue T-shirt is _____

③ Gino's café is good. Harry's café is better.

Harry's cafe is _____

④ My sister isn't good at languages. I am worse.

I am _____

⑤ The red pen is $7. The blue one is $5.

The blue pen is _____

18.6 LEE LA POSTAL Y ESCRIBE LAS RESPUESTAS A LAS PREGUNTAS EN FRASES COMPLETAS

Which city is more expensive, Paris or Rome?

Paris is more expensive than Rome.

1 Which is better, the food in Paris or at home?

_____

2 Where did Pat eat the best meal?

_____

3 What is the tallest building in Paris?

_____

4 Where can you hear the best music in Paris?

_____

5 What's the most famous painting in the Louvre?

_____

Dear Kim,

Bonjour! Paris is much more expensive than Rome. The food here is much better than at home. I had the best meal ever at La Coupole last night. I visited the Eiffel Tower on the weekend. Did you know it's the tallest building in the city? I went to Le Pompon on Thursday. It has the best music in Paris. On Sunday I went to the Louvre. There is a lot there, but its most famous painting is the Mona Lisa.

Love,

Pat

18.7 DI LAS FRASES EN VOZ ALTA, COMPLETANDO LOS ESPACIOS

Anna _____ *is the best* _____ (good) driver in her family.

1 Rhode Island _____ (small) state in the US.

2 The Humber Bridge _____ (long) than the Severn Bridge.

3 George _____ (bad) student in the class.

4 A Ferrari _____ (expensive) than a Fiat car.

5 Saturn _____ (far) from Earth than Mars.

19 Utilizar números grandes

Habitualmente, escribimos los números mayores de 100 en cifras. Al pronunciarlos, añade "and" delante de las dos últimas cifras, por ejemplo, "one hundred and ten".

⚙ **Lenguaje** Números grandes
Aa **Vocabulario** Millares y millones
🧩 **Habilidad** Hablar de números grandes

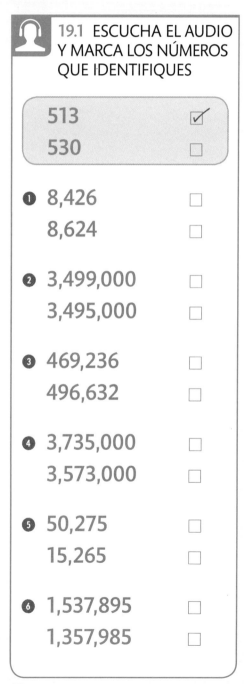

19.1 ESCUCHA EL AUDIO Y MARCA LOS NÚMEROS QUE IDENTIFIQUES

513	☑
530	☐

① 8,426 ☐
8,624 ☐

② 3,499,000 ☐
3,495,000 ☐

③ 469,236 ☐
496,632 ☐

④ 3,735,000 ☐
3,573,000 ☐

⑤ 50,275 ☐
15,265 ☐

⑥ 1,537,895 ☐
1,357,985 ☐

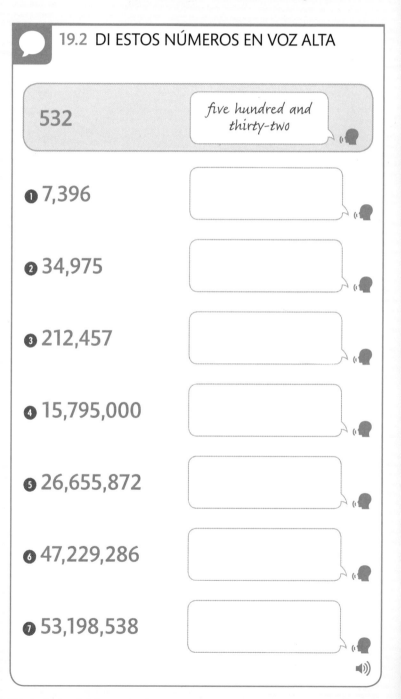

19.2 DI ESTOS NÚMEROS EN VOZ ALTA

532 — *five hundred and thirty-two*

① 7,396

② 34,975

③ 212,457

④ 15,795,000

⑤ 26,655,872

⑥ 47,229,286

⑦ 53,198,538

19.3 ESCRIBE LOS NÚMEROS EN CIFRAS

Five million, two thousand, seven hundred and fifty-six	= _5,002,756_

❶ Four hundred and fifty-five thousand and fifty-eight = _____

❷ Five hundred and sixty-four thousand, one hundred and forty-three = _____

❸ Three thousand, six hundred and eighty-two = _____

❹ Forty-five million, seven hundred and twelve thousand, six hundred = _____

❺ Sixty-three thousand, eight hundred and fifty-nine = _____

❻ Nine hundred and fifty thousand, eight hundred and thirty-seven = _____

❼ Twenty-three million, one hundred thousand, two hundred and sixty-nine = _____

❽ Nine hundred and seventy-eight = _____

❾ One hundred and eighty-five thousand, seven hundred and ninety-four = _____

❿ Fifty million, two hundred and twelve thousand, seven hundred and five = _____

⓫ Ten million, four hundred and sixty thousand, two hundred and forty = _____

⓬ Three hundred and thirty-six thousand, four hundred and twenty-two = _____

⓭ Sixteen thousand, seven hundred and three = _____

⓮ One million, three hundred and fifty-nine thousand, six hundred and seven = _____

🔊

19.4 ESCUCHA EL AUDIO Y ESCRIBE LOS NÚMEROS QUE IDENTIFIQUES

_73,245_

❶ _____
❷ _____
❸ _____
❹ _____

❺ _____
❻ _____
❼ _____
❽ _____
❾ _____

❿ _____
⓫ _____
⓬ _____
⓭ _____
⓮ _____

Aa 20.1 EL CALENDARIO ESCRIBE LAS PALABRAS DEL RECUADRO BAJO SU IMAGEN

SAT — *Saturday*

SUN — 1 _____

MON — 2 _____

TUE — 3 _____

WED — 4 _____

THU — 5 _____

FRI — 6 _____

7 _____

8 _____

9 _____

10 _____

Feb — 11 _____

Apr — 12 _____

Jul — 13 _____

Aug — 14 _____

Sept — 15 _____

Nov — 16 _____

Dec — 17 _____

18 _____

19 _____

December	summer	August	month	July	April	Wednesday
winter	Friday	week	~~Saturday~~	September	Thursday	day
February	November	fortnight	Sunday	Tuesday	Monday

Aa 20.2 **NÚMEROS** ESCRIBE LAS PALABRAS DEL RECUADRO BAJO LOS NÚMEROS CORRECTOS

2nd
second

19th
❶ _____

26th
❷ _____

5th
❸ _____

6th
❹ _____

29th
❺ _____

21st
❻ _____

16th
❼ _____

27th
❽ _____

17th
❾ _____

10th
❿ _____

14th
⓫ _____

1st
⓬ _____

11th
⓭ _____

20th
⓮ _____

23rd
⓯ _____

31st
⓰ _____

7th
⓱ _____

3rd
⓲ _____

4th
⓳ _____

---

second   twenty-third   twenty-ninth   twenty-seventh

twenty-first   ninteenth   twenty-sixth   thirty-first   fifth   seventh

seventeenth   twentieth   tenth   sixteenth   first

third   eleventh   fourth   fourteenth   sixth

Hablar de fechas

Existen dos formas distintas de escribir y decir fechas. Utilizas los números junto con el mes para indicar de qué fecha estás hablando.

⚙️ **Lenguaje** Fechas, "was born" y "ago"
Aa Vocabulario Números, meses y años
🧩 **Habilidad** Hablar de fechas

21.1 ESCRIBE CADA FRASE EN SU OTRA FORMA

NOTA
Escribe la fecha en la forma "May 2" en EE.UU. y como "2nd of May" en el Reino Unido.

Sally arrives on the 4th of August.	*Sally arrives on August 4.*

① _____ We returned on September 9.

② Sarah was born on the 12th of March. _____

③ _____ Greg was born on February 12.

④ My birthday is on the 22nd of November. _____

⑤ _____ I stop working on July 21.

⑥ The year begins on the 1st of January. _____

21.2 ESCUCHA EL AUDIO Y RESPONDE A LAS PREGUNTAS

Claire y Phil discuten una fecha para reunirse.

On November 23, Claire...
- **is meeting a colleague.** ☐
- **is meeting a client.** ☑
- **is not at work.** ☐

❷ On November 25, Claire...
- **is going to Seattle.** ☐
- **is on vacation.** ☐
- **is going to Los Angeles.** ☐

❶ On November 24, Phil...
- **is not at work.** ☐
- **has another meeting.** ☐
- **is visiting the factory.** ☐

❸ On November 26, Phil...
- **is free all day.** ☐
- **is busy all day.** ☐
- **is in Los Angeles.** ☐

21.3 LEE EL ARTÍCULO Y RESPONDE A LAS PREGUNTAS

Clarissa was born in 1980.
True ☐ **False** ☐ **Not given** ✓

❶ She was born in New York City.
True ☐ **False** ☐ **Not given** ☐

❷ Clarissa became famous in the 1980s.
True ☐ **False** ☐ **Not given** ☐

❸ Heaven's Child released five albums.
True ☐ **False** ☐ **Not given** ☐

❹ Her first album was called *Clarissa*.
True ☐ **False** ☐ **Not given** ☐

❺ She released *Clarissa* in 2012.
True ☐ **False** ☐ **Not given** ☐

❻ She has released a perfume.
True ☐ **False** ☐ **Not given** ☐

❼ She was 25 when she married a singer.
True ☐ **False** ☐ **Not given** ☐

ENTERTAINMENT

Singing sensation

Clarissa's rise to fame

Clarissa was born in New York City in 1985. She is one of the most successful singers in the world. She became famous in the 1990s when she started singing professionally.

Her first solo album was *Carried Away*. Clarissa released it in 2005, when she was 20 years old. The album won lots of awards, including five Best Singer of the Year Awards. She has released seven more albums, including *Clarissa* in 2012, which sold 15 million copies.

Clarissa has starred in lots of movies, and played a singer in *Supergirls* in 2006. She also released a perfume in 2012.

She married a singer in 2008, when she was 23. They had a child in 2011.

21.4 UTILIZA EL DIAGRAMA PARA CREAR OCHO FRASES CORRECTAS Y DILAS EN VOZ ALTA

My wedding is on February 16.

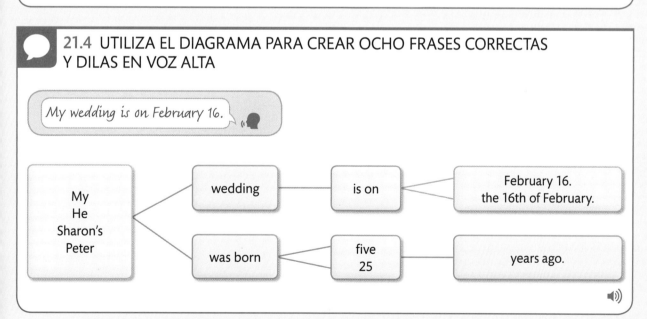

| My He Sharon's Peter | wedding | is on | February 16. the 16th of February. |
| | was born | five 25 | years ago. |

22 Hablar del pasado

El past simple sirve para hablar de hechos que pasaron en un momento definido del pasado, o el estado de algo en un momento determinado.

⚙ **Lenguaje** Past simple de "to be"
Aa **Vocabulario** Trabajos, ciudad y acontecimientos
🧩 **Habilidad** Hablar de situaciones del pasado

 22.1 TACHA LA PALABRA INCORRECTA DE CADA FRASE

You ~~was~~ / were at the museum this afternoon.

1. Roberta was / were at the party last night.

2. We was / were in college together.

3. You was / were a student at that time.

4. There was / were lots of people in town.

5. They was / were there in the evening.

6. Your friends was / were at the museum yesterday.

7. She was / were a teacher in the 1970s.

8. There was / were a café near the beach.

9. My mom was / were a dentist.

10. Chris and I was / were happy about the news.

11. They was / were at the theater last night.

12. Frank was / were an actor in the 1990s.

13. It was / were very cold in Norway.

14. My parents was / were away last week.

15. We was / were in Los Angeles in 2014.

16. You was / were at the movie theater on Friday.

17. Jenny was / were a nurse for 20 years.

🔊

 22.2 ESCUCHA EL AUDIO Y RELACIONA LOS AÑOS CON LOS ACONTECIMIENTOS CORRECTOS

Charles Dickens was a popular writer.

1. Crackle was the most successful pop group.

2. Charis Rose was a famous movie star.

3. Leonardo Da Vinci was a successful artist.

4. Shakespeare lived in London.

| 1960s | 1840s | 1490s | 1605 | 1910s |

68

22.3 LEE EL CORREO Y RESPONDE A LAS PREGUNTAS

✉

To: Mick

Subject: My trip to Dublin

Hi Mick,

How are you? I was in Dublin last week with my friend Janet. It's a beautiful city. You should visit some day!
We were at Dublin Castle. Do you know it? It's very old, and was built in 1204. The weather wasn't so good while
we were there. It was cold and it rained a lot. There were lots of people there, though!
We were on Grafton Street where there were lots of stores, and some nice cafes, too. When we were in a traditional
Irish bar, I drank some Guinness.
On Friday, we were at the Botanical Gardens. It was so beautiful there.

See you soon,
Cath

Cath was in Dubai last weekend.	**True** ☐	**False** ☑

❶ Cath was in Dublin with her friend Jane. **True** ☐ **False** ☐

❷ She visited the cathedral. **True** ☐ **False** ☐

❸ Dublin Castle was built in 1204. **True** ☐ **False** ☐

❹ The weather was bad. **True** ☐ **False** ☐

❺ There weren't many people. **True** ☐ **False** ☐

❻ There were museums on Grafton Street. **True** ☐ **False** ☐

❼ They were in an Irish bar. **True** ☐ **False** ☐

❽ Cath drank Guinness in Dublin. **True** ☐ **False** ☐

❾ They were at Dublin Zoo. **True** ☐ **False** ☐

❿ On Thursday, they were at the Botanical Gardens. **True** ☐ **False** ☐

22.4 TACHA LA PALABRA INCORRECTA DE CADA FRASE

They ~~wasn't~~ / weren't very good at science.

1 It wasn't / weren't an interesting book.

2 There wasn't / weren't any good movies on.

3 We wasn't / weren't in the US in 2012.

4 Glen wasn't / weren't at home when I called.

5 There wasn't / weren't a theater in my town.

6 Trevor wasn't / weren't in Berlin in 1994.

7 There wasn't / weren't a library in the town.

8 We wasn't / weren't at home last night.

9 Peter wasn't / weren't a student at Harvard.

10 Carlo wasn't / weren't very good at singing.

11 Meg and Clive wasn't / weren't teachers then.

12 They wasn't / weren't at the restaurant last night.

◀))

22.5 ESCRIBE LAS FRASES EN SU FORMA NEGATIVA

She was a very good teacher.
She wasn't a very good teacher.

1 Brad was a teacher in 2012.

_____

2 The weather was bad.

_____

3 It was a comfortable bed.

_____

4 They were interesting people.

_____

5 Brendan's parents were doctors.

_____

6 Pete and Sue were on the beach all day.

_____

◀))

22.6 VUELVE A ESCRIBIR LAS FRASES PONIENDO LAS PALABRAS EN SU ORDEN CORRECTO

| weren't | There | cafés. | good | any |
There weren't any good cafés.
_____

1 | 30 | was | Simon | an actor | years. | for |
_____

2 | was | really | It | in | Canada. | cold |
_____

3 | the | town? | there | any | in | Were | stores |
_____

4 | dancing. | Phil | at | good | wasn't |
_____

5 | Rebecca | in | Was | in | 2010? | Arizona |
_____

◀))

22.7 HAZ PREGUNTAS QUE CORRESPONDAN A LAS AFIRMACIONES Y DILAS EN VOZ ALTA

They were late for the English lesson.

> *Were they late for the English lesson?*

① She was at school in the nineties.

② You were at the park last Sunday.

③ There were lots of people at his party.

④ He was very good at playing soccer.

⑤ James was at work until 8 o'clock yesterday.

⑥ You were at the airport before me.

⑦ They were at Simon's wedding last week.

⑧ We were in Spain for two weeks.

⑨ Hayley was happy in college.

22.8 UTILIZA EL DIAGRAMA PARA CREAR NUEVE FRASES CORRECTAS Y DILAS EN VOZ ALTA

> *Was she a teacher?*

| Was / Were | she / they / there / you | a teacher? / angry? / a party last night? / at home yesterday? |

Hechos del pasado

Algunos verbos tienen una forma regular en past simple. Puedes usarlos para hablar de la semana pasada, el año pasado o de tu vida. Sus formas en past simple acaban en "ed".

🔧 **Lenguaje** Verbos regulares en past simple
Aa Vocabulario Aficiones y sucesos de la vida
Habilidad Hablar del pasado

🔧 23.1 COMPLETA LOS ESPACIOS PONIENDO LOS VERBOS EN PAST SIMPLE

Gary ___played___ (play) soccer last night.

1 Roger _____ (watch) the game.

2 They _____ (call) their dad yesterday.

3 We _____ (arrive) at the hotel at 7pm.

4 They _____ (walk) to school yesterday.

5 Simon _____ (work) late last week.

6 My mother _____ (dance) at the party.

7 They _____ (wash) their new car.

8 Terry _____ (study) French at school.

9 Karen _____ (travel) to Africa.

🔊

🔧 23.2 COMPLETA LOS ESPACIOS Y ESCRIBE LO OPUESTO DE CADA FRASE

I **cooked** dinner last night.	I didn't cook dinner last night.
1 _____	Craig didn't **phone** his girlfriend.
2 The doctor **visited** my grandmother.	_____
3 _____	We didn't **play** tennis last night.
4 My sister **walked** to the shops.	_____
5 _____	They didn't **watch** TV last night.
6 Debbie **moved** to the US this year.	_____
7 _____	David didn't **clean** his room again.

23.3 COMPLETA LOS ESPACIOS CON LAS PALABRAS DEL RECUADRO

Chris _____*danced*_____ at the party.

1 Kelly _____ TV last night.

2 Tim _____ home on Friday.

3 Ed _____ as a waiter last year.

4 I _____ some Mexican food.

5 Marge _____ her sister last night.

6 Marion _____ some music.

7 The children _____ a question.

8 My dad _____ in Canada.

9 They _____ my birthday.

worked	remembered	asked	played	lived
walked	watched	tried	~~danced~~	called

Aa 23.4 BUSCA EN LA TABLA NUEVE VERBOS EN PAST SIMPLE Y ORDÉNALOS SEGÚN SU NORMA DE FORMACIÓN

```
E L S T A R T E D A M A T
Y Q F V R E Z C S E O E A
E M S N K V R A N R V C C
A R R I V E D L Y F E H V
O V L N E R X K T P D Z R
G E A W A S H E D D N S L
R D O R V T G F Q V I Z E
O A I C N U Y Y E I B T K
N N D T M D E M S S A S E
O C A R R I E D E I A S J
G E E I E E D R M T T O W
A D R E H D L G O E M N A
A G I D X R K R C D O A R
```

VERBOS QUE AÑADEN "-ED"

1 *washed* _____

2 _____

3 _____

VERBOS QUE AÑADEN "-IED"

4 *studied* _____

5 _____

6 _____

VERBOS QUE AÑADEN "-D"

7 *danced* _____

8 _____

9 _____

73

23.5 VUELVE A ESCRIBIR ESTAS FRASES EN PAST SIMPLE

> They watch TV together yesterday.
> _They watched TV together yesterday._

1 I study English.

_____

2 Jim arrives today.

_____

3 My son carries my bags.

_____

4 She dances very well.

_____

5 Bill washes his socks.

_____

23.6 LEE EL BLOG Y RESPONDE A LAS PREGUNTAS

On Monday, Zoe...
finished work early.	☐
worked late.	☑
watched a movie with her boyfriend.	☐

1 On Tuesday, Zoe...
visited an old friend.	☐
cooked a delicious dinner.	☐
cleaned her kitchen.	☐

2 On Tuesday evening, she...
watched TV with her boyfriend.	☐
listened to the radio.	☐
started a new book.	☐

3 On Wednesday, she...
visited her grandmother.	☐
saw her friend and listened to music.	☐
painted the bathroom.	☐

4 On Thursday, Zoe...
listened to the radio with a friend.	☐
danced at a party.	☐
washed the floors.	☐

Zoe's zone

HOME | ENTRIES | ABOUT | CONTACT

POSTED TUESDAY, MARCH 23

A BUSY WEEK

I'm sorry for not posting anything for a few days, but I was so busy last week.

On Monday, I worked at the restaurant until 1am. There was a big birthday party with lots of guests, and I only arrived home at 2am!

Tuesday was a bit better. I stayed at home and did some housework. I cleaned the kitchen and washed the floors. In the evening I watched a film on the TV with my boyfriend.

On Wednesday, I visited my grandmother. We walked by the river near her house. In the evening, she cooked a delicious dinner and we listened to some music.

On Thursday, my sister invited me to a party at her friend's. It was great. We danced all night!

23.7 ESCUCHA EL AUDIO Y CONECTA EL INICIO Y EL FINAL DE CADA FRASE

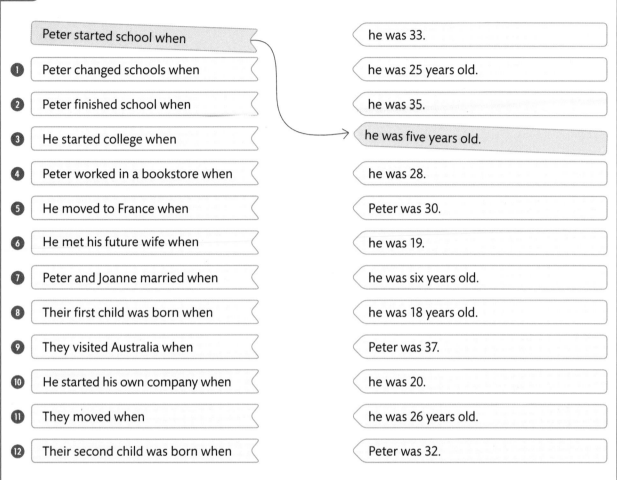

	Peter started school when		he was 33.
❶	Peter changed schools when		he was 25 years old.
❷	Peter finished school when		he was 35.
❸	He started college when		he was five years old.
❹	Peter worked in a bookstore when		he was 28.
❺	He moved to France when		Peter was 30.
❻	He met his future wife when		he was 19.
❼	Peter and Joanne married when		he was six years old.
❽	Their first child was born when		he was 18 years old.
❾	They visited Australia when		Peter was 37.
❿	He started his own company when		he was 20.
⓫	They moved when		he was 26 years old.
⓬	Their second child was born when		Peter was 32.

23.8 UTILIZA EL DIAGRAMA PARA CREAR NUEVE FRASES CORRECTAS Y DILAS EN VOZ ALTA

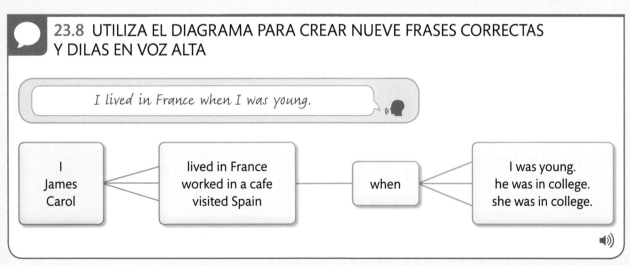

I lived in France when I was young.

| I
James
Carol | lived in France
worked in a cafe
visited Spain | when | I was young.
he was in college.
she was in college. |

24 Habilidades del pasado

En el past simple, "can" se convierte en "could".
A menudo se utiliza para hablar de aquello que
podías hacer en el pasado, pero ya no.

⚙ **Lenguaje** Utilizar "could" en past simple
Aa Vocabulario Habilidades y aficiones
🏃 **Habilidad** Hablar de tus habilidades pasadas

24.1 VUELVE A ESCRIBIR LAS FRASES EN PAST TENSE UTILIZANDO "COULD"

Jimmy **can** cook Italian food.   *Jimmy could cook Italian food.*

1 Carl **can** run fast.

2 Brendan **can** speak five languages.

3 Sally **can** paint beautifully.

4 Rob and Sarah **can't** dance flamenco.

5 Yasmin **can** climb a tree.

6 Danny **can** drive a bus.

7 We **can't** ride a horse.

8 Jenny **can** play the violin.

9 Ben **can** fly a plane.

10 Yuna **can** speak Italian.

24.2 UTILIZA EL DIAGRAMA PARA CREAR 18 FRASES CORRECTAS Y DILAS EN VOZ ALTA

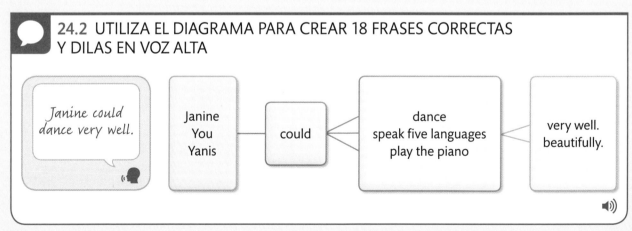

Janine could dance very well.

| Janine You Yanis | could | dance speak five languages play the piano | very well. beautifully. |

24.3 ESCUCHA EL AUDIO Y RESPONDE A LAS PREGUNTAS

Seis personas hablan sobre aptitudes y habilidades.

When Sandra was one, she could...
walk. ☑
speak. ☐
read. ☐

1 Martha could play the violin when she was...
six. ☐
seven. ☐
eight. ☐

2 James could paint well when he was...
three years old. ☐
seven years old. ☐
12 years old. ☐

3 When Max was young he could speak...
seven languages. ☐
six languages. ☐
five languages. ☐

4 Winnie's grandmother could...
paint beautifully. ☐
bake cakes. ☐
dance salsa. ☐

5 When Alfie was a child he could...
climb a tree. ☐
climb a mountain. ☐
run very fast. ☐

24.4 VUELVE A ESCRIBIR LAS FRASES PONIENDO LAS PALABRAS EN SU ORDEN CORRECTO

When | was | couldn't | swim. | I | five | I

When I was five I couldn't swim.

1 swim | was | Greg | when | he | four. | could

_____

2 to | couldn't | the | come | party. | Simon

_____

3 speak | could | Jean | Japanese.

_____

4 dog | very | could | My | quickly. | run

_____

5 could | fluent | Greg | Russian. | speak

_____

6 couldn't | I | the | snow. | because | of | drive

_____

7 find | street. | couldn't | We | your

_____

77

Aa 25.1 ENTRETENIMIENTO ESCRIBE LAS PALABRAS DEL RECUADRO BAJO SU IMAGEN

movie star

1 _____

2 _____

3 _____

6 _____

7 _____

8 _____

9 _____

12 _____

13 _____

14 _____

15 _____

18 _____

19 _____

20 _____

21 _____

④ _____

⑤ _____

⑩ _____

⑪ _____

⑯ _____

⑰ _____

㉒ _____

㉓ _____

novel   TV show   bookstore

romance   horror

~~movie star~~   clap   science fiction

thriller   exhibition

play   documentary   author

newspaper   villain   movie

hero   action

musical   director   comedy

audience   crime

main character

Algunos verbos tienen una forma irregular en past simple. Sus formas de past simple no se forman de acuerdo con las reglas habituales, y a veces son muy distintas del infinitivo.

✿ **Lenguaje** Verbos irregulares en past simple
Aa **Vocabulario** Adverbios de secuencia
🧩 **Habilidad** Hablar del pasado

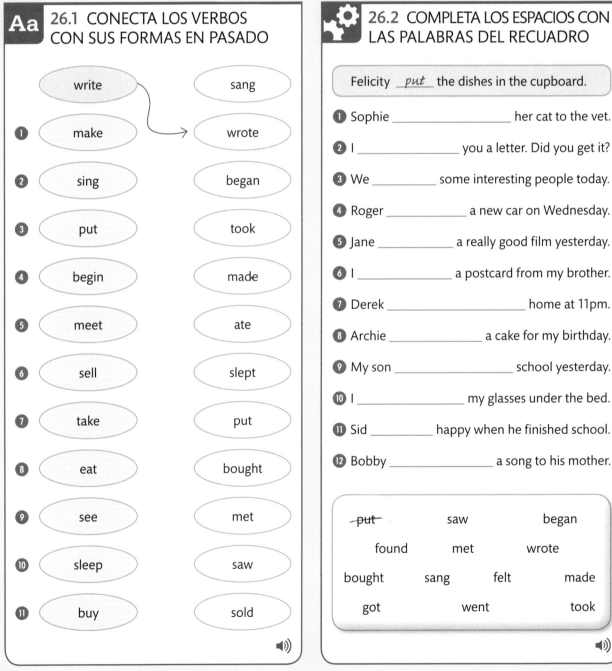

Aa 26.1 CONECTA LOS VERBOS CON SUS FORMAS EN PASADO

write ⟶ wrote

1. make — sang
2. sing — began
3. put — took
4. begin — made
5. meet — ate
6. sell — slept
7. take — put
8. eat — bought
9. see — met
10. sleep — saw
11. buy — sold

⚙ 26.2 COMPLETA LOS ESPACIOS CON LAS PALABRAS DEL RECUADRO

Felicity _put_ the dishes in the cupboard.

1. Sophie _____ her cat to the vet.
2. I _____ you a letter. Did you get it?
3. We _____ some interesting people today.
4. Roger _____ a new car on Wednesday.
5. Jane _____ a really good film yesterday.
6. I _____ a postcard from my brother.
7. Derek _____ home at 11pm.
8. Archie _____ a cake for my birthday.
9. My son _____ school yesterday.
10. I _____ my glasses under the bed.
11. Sid _____ happy when he finished school.
12. Bobby _____ a song to his mother.

~~put~~	saw	began
found	met	wrote
bought	sang	felt	made
got	went	took

26.3 COMPLETA LOS ESPACIOS PONIENDO LOS VERBOS EN PAST SIMPLE

Selma _____broke_____ (break) the classroom window while playing with her friends.

❶ Samantha and Cathy _____ (eat) pizza after work.

❷ Katy _____ (go) to the disco with Ben on Friday night.

❸ Miguel _____ (write) a beautiful song about his wife Christine.

❹ Pauline and Emma _____ (get) lots of presents for Christmas this year.

❺ The kids _____ (see) a play at the theater with us last week.

❻ Keith _____ (buy) a new guitar for his brother Patrick on his birthday.

❼ Emily _____ (sleep) in a tent in the back yard last night.

❽ Pablo _____ (sing) a traditional song at Elma and Mark's wedding.

❾ Tammy _____ (sell) her old computer to her neighbor Anna.

❿ They _____ (feel) sad after watching the film about a boy who lost his dog.

⓫ Mick _____ (begin) to read a new book yesterday evening.

⓬ Joan _____ (find) a gold necklace in the garden while she was gardening.

⓭ We _____ (take) the children to the movie theater next to the shopping mall.

⓮ Warren _____ (make) a delicious sandwich for his daughter's lunch.

26.4 COMPLETA LOS ESPACIOS UTILIZANDO LAS PALABRAS DEL RECUADRO

I had a shower. _____Then_____ I had breakfast with my family.

❶ _____ , Bob ate some soup. Then he had a burger and a sandwich.

❷ My cousins have stayed for six weeks! They've _____ decided to go home.

❸ First, I went to the baker's. _____ , I went to the butcher's next door.

❹ Samantha gave me a letter. _____ , she left to go back home.

| first | next | ~~then~~ | finally | after that |

Aa 26.5 RELACIONA LAS PREGUNTAS CON SUS RESPUESTAS

Did you go to the party?

❶ Did Samantha take her money?

❷ Did you get some bread?

❸ Did you meet Rebecca's boyfriend?

❹ Did you find your glasses?

❺ Did you see any tigers?

❻ Did Dan buy a new car?

❼ Did you go to the movies?

❽ Did Jim make that cake?

❾ Did Billy eat his dinner?

❿ Did you write him a letter?

⓫ Did you sell your house?

⓬ Did you begin your course?

⓭ Did you sleep well?

Yes, he's really handsome.

No, it was too expensive.

Yes, I had a great time.

No, the zoo was closed.

No, there were no good movies on.

Yes, he ate everything.

Yes, we're moving on Saturday.

No, it starts on Wednesday.

No, I sent him a text.

Sorry, the baker was closed.

No, it was too noisy in my room.

No, he bought it at the baker's.

No, she left it on the table.

Yes, they were in the bathroom.

26.6 VUELVE A ESCRIBIR LAS AFIRMACIONES COMO PREGUNTAS SIMPLES UTILIZANDO "DID"

> They went to the beach by bus.
>
> How *did they go to the beach?* _____

1 I saw a horror film at the movie theater.

What _____

2 Sarah took Phil to the wedding party.

Who _____

3 We had a pizza for dinner on Friday.

What _____

4 They went to New Zealand on vacation.

Where _____

5 Steve bought a new cellphone.

What _____

6 Jim ate fish and chips for lunch.

What _____

7 Kelly met her sister last week.

Who _____

8 Peter put his phone in the drawer.

Where _____

9 I found your watch in the garden.

Where _____

10 Anna made a sandwich for lunch.

What _____

11 I got a necklace from Doug.

What _____

12 Peter sang a rock song for Elma.

What _____

13 My sister came to see me yesterday.

When _____

🔊

Aa 26.7 ESCRIBE LOS VERBOS EN LA PARRILLA EN SU FORMA PAST SIMPLE

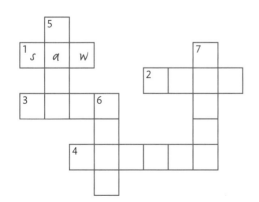

HORIZONTAL	VERTICAL
1 See	**5** Make
2 Sell	**6** Take
3 Feel	**7** Sleep
4 Buy	

Aa 27.1 HERRAMIENTAS ESCRIBE LAS PALABRAS DEL RECUADRO BAJO SU IMAGEN

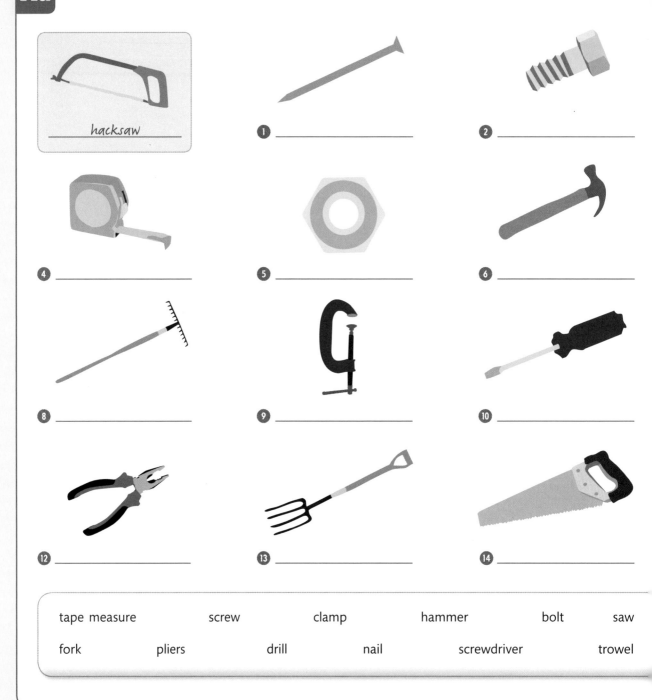

hacksaw

❶ _____

❷ _____

❹ _____

❺ _____

❻ _____

❽ _____

❾ _____

❿ _____

⓬ _____

⓭ _____

⓮ _____

tape measure	screw	clamp	hammer	bolt	saw
fork	pliers	drill	nail	screwdriver	trowel

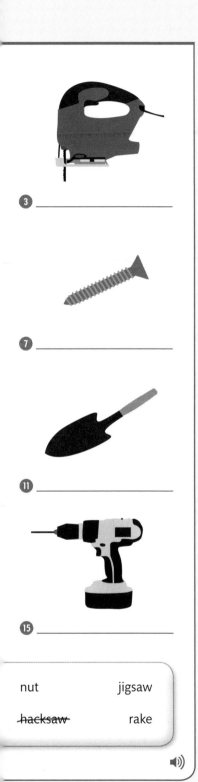

3 _____

7 _____

11 _____

15 _____

nut   jigsaw

~~hacksaw~~   rake

Aa **27.2 INSTRUMENTOS DE COCINA** ESCRIBE LAS PALABRAS DEL RECUADRO BAJO SU IMAGEN

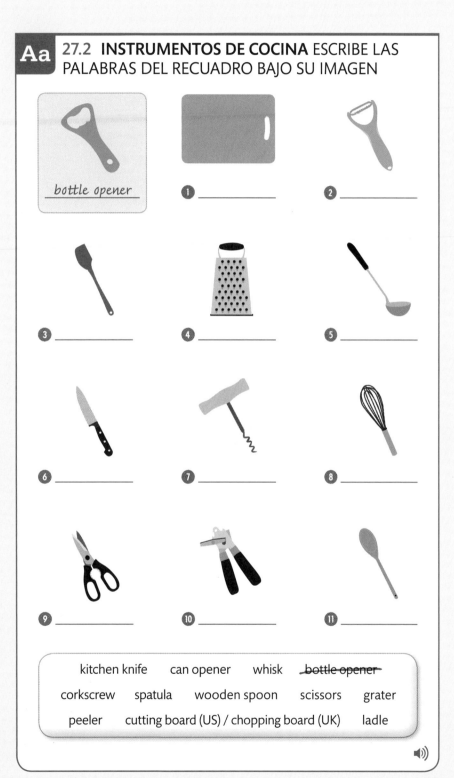

bottle opener

1 _____

2 _____

3 _____

4 _____

5 _____

6 _____

7 _____

8 _____

9 _____

10 _____

11 _____

kitchen knife   can opener   whisk   ~~bottle opener~~

corkscrew   spatula   wooden spoon   scissors   grater

peeler   cutting board (US) / chopping board (UK)   ladle

28 Contar una historia

Puedes utilizar "about" para hablar del argumento de películas, espectáculos o historias. Utiliza adjetivos para que tu descripción sea más específica.

⚙ **Lenguaje** "About", opiniones
Aa Vocabulario Opiniones
🧩 **Habilidad** Hablar de los medios y la cultura

Aa 28.1 BUSCA SIETE ADJETIVOS EN LA TABLA Y ESCRÍBELOS EN LA LISTA CORRECTA

```
S  G  N  I  D  X  D  T  R  B
L  E  K  B  L  E  O  H  Y  O
O  D  R  M  J  A  J  R  S  R
W  K  N  S  I  Q  Y  I  R  I
F  U  N  N  Y  Y  E  L  B  N
E  D  I  S  R  B  R  L  Y  G
M  C  O  N  F  U  S  I  N  G
S  I  L  L  Y  N  S  N  N  V
E  X  C  I  T  I  N  G  N  D
```

OPINIÓN POSITIVA

1. _funny_

2. _____

3. _____

OPINIÓN NEGATIVA

4. _boring_

5. _____

6. _____

7. _____

Aa 28.2 CONECTA LAS IMÁGENES CON SUS DESCRIPCIONES

It's a book about two young sisters from the country.

1. It's a thriller about two police officers.

2. It's a story about London in the 1890s.

3. It's a movie about a racing car driver.

4. It's a musical about a couple who got married.

5. It's a movie about two brothers.

🔊

28.3 LEE LA RESEÑA DE CINE Y RESPONDE A LAS PREGUNTAS

Films on Friday

HOME | ENTRIES | ABOUT | CONTACT

 Films out this Friday

Bankbreakers is a film about some friends who decide to rob a bank. They use the internet to find which banks in Europe hold the most money and valuable items. First they go to a bank in Munich, turn off the alarms, and steal some money and jewelry. After a successful robbery, the thieves decide to rob another bank in Paris. This time, they get caught by video surveillance cameras and they go to prison. I didn't enjoy the film. I thought it was a bit slow and not very well acted. *The King* is a film version of the Shakespeare play *Macbeth*. After a big battle, Macbeth meets three witches who tell him he will become Thane of Cawdor and then king. Although King Duncan gives Macbeth the title of Thane of Cawdor, Macbeth and his wife plot to kill him. I thought the film was thrilling because the story is exciting. I liked it a lot.

> What is the film *Bankbreakers* about?
>
> *It's about some friends who rob a bank.*

❶ Where is the first bank they rob?

_____

❷ How do they get into the first bank?

_____

❸ How are the thieves caught?

_____

❹ What happens to them after they are caught?

_____

❺ What does the reviewer think of this film?

_____

❻ What is the film *The King* based on?

_____

❼ Who does Macbeth meet after a big battle?

_____

❽ What does King Duncan give Macbeth?

_____

❾ Who does Macbeth plot with?

_____

❿ Who does Macbeth kill?

_____

⓫ What does the reviewer think of this film?

_____

28.4 ESCUCHA EL AUDIO Y NUMERA LAS FRASES EN EL ORDEN EN QUE LAS ESCUCHES

 Unos amigos hablan sobre libros que han leído y películas, obras teatrales y musicales que han visto.

A The play was about a hairdresser. ☐

B The book was about some jewelry thieves. ☐

C The couple in the film wanted a divorce. ☐ 1

D The musical was called *Seven Days in Heaven*. ☐

E The story is about an adventure kids went on. ☐

F The film was about King George the Sixth. ☐

28.5 VUELVE A ESCRIBIR LAS FRASES CORRIGIENDO LOS ERRORES

> I **enjoys** the play. It was thrilling.
> *I enjoyed the play. It was thrilling.*

1 Jo **didn't enjoyed** the show because it was boring.

2 Hannah **didn't like** the film because it was fun.

3 I **hate** the musical because the story was silly.

4 He enjoyed the play because it was **thrilled**.

5 I **liked** the play because it was boring.

6 Paul hated the show because it was **scared**.

7 I **hates** the show because it was slow.

8 She liked the story because it was **romance**.

9 He **enjoys** the movie because it was exciting.

10 I hated the play because it was **bored**.

11 He **doesn't enjoy** the film because it was scary.

12 She liked the book because it was **excited**.

13 I **don't like** the play because it was silly.

14 The movie was **thrilled** and they loved it.

15 I **enjoys** the musical because it was romantic.

🔊

28.6 VUELVE A ESCRIBIR LAS FRASES PONIENDO LAS PALABRAS EN SU ORDEN CORRECTO

| funny. | I | opera | because | it | was | loved | the |

I loved the opera because it was funny.

1 | it | silly. | hated | musical | because | was | I | the |
_____

2 | thrilling. | loved | film | was | Anna | it | the | because |
_____

3 | the | Tom | it | didn't | slow. | movie | because | enjoy | was |
_____

4 | it | enjoyed | because | the | was | Sam | film | funny. |
_____

5 | because | a | Kay | book | had | it | romantic ending. | loved | the |
_____

6 | the | boring. | was | hated | because | it | Jim | show |
_____

7 | was | it | I | really liked | play | because | thrilling. | the |
_____

8 | the | scary. | I | like | book | was | it | didn't | because |
_____

9 | was | to understand. | it | didn't | the | because | difficult | I | enjoy | opera |
_____

10 | the | had | enjoyed | because | story. | it | an | book | They | exciting |
_____

29 Preguntar sobre el pasado

Puedes hacer preguntas sobre el pasado utilizando "did". Resulta útil para preguntar sobre hechos pasados, como viajes o vacaciones.

⚙ **Lenguaje** Preguntas en past simple
Aa Vocabulario Viajes y actividades
Habilidad Hablar de las vacaciones

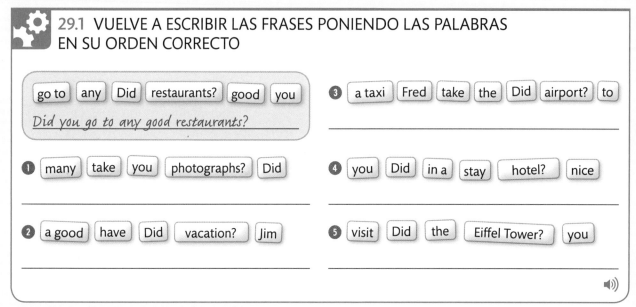

⚙ 29.1 VUELVE A ESCRIBIR LAS FRASES PONIENDO LAS PALABRAS EN SU ORDEN CORRECTO

go to | any | Did | restaurants? | good | you
Did you go to any good restaurants?

❸ a taxi | Fred | take | the | Did | airport? | to
_____

❶ many | take | you | photographs? | Did
_____

❹ you | Did | in a | stay | hotel? | nice
_____

❷ a good | have | Did | vacation? | Jim
_____

❺ visit | Did | the | Eiffel Tower? | you
_____

🔊

⚙ 29.2 VUELVE A ESCRIBIR LAS FRASES EN FORMA DE PREGUNTA

They went walking in Austria.
Did they go walking in Austria?

❶ They saw some crocodiles.
_____

❷ We ate some Indian food.
_____

❸ Paul sailed to Corfu.
_____

❹ Your sister went skiing in the Alps.
_____

❺ Chris stayed in a cheap hotel.
_____

❻ My mom went waterskiing.
_____

❼ We visited some beautiful beaches.
_____

❽ We bought some presents for the kids.
_____

❾ Bob and Sally had pizza for lunch.
_____

🔊

29.3 ESCUCHA EL AUDIO Y MARCA SI CADA COSA HA PASADO O NO

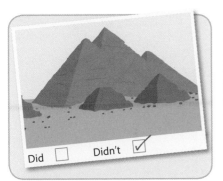

Did ☐   Didn't ☑

1 Did ☐   Didn't ☐

2 Did ☐   Didn't ☐

3 Did ☐   Didn't ☐

4 Did ☐   Didn't ☐

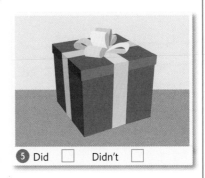

5 Did ☐   Didn't ☐

29.4 ESCUCHA DE NUEVO EL AUDIO Y RESPONDE A LAS PREGUNTAS CON RESPUESTAS CORTAS

Did Simon visit Egypt?
No, he didn't.

1 Did Simon visit Italy?

_____

2 Did it rain?

_____

3 Did Simon visit Pisa?

_____

4 Did Simon visit Rome?

_____

5 Did Simon like the food in Italy?

_____

6 Did Simon and Carol go waterskiing?

_____

7 Did Carol like waterskiing?

_____

8 Did Simon like waterskiing?

_____

9 Did Simon buy Carly a present?

_____

29.5 CONECTA LAS PREGUNTAS CON SUS CORRESPONDIENTES RESPUESTAS

Why did you go there?	→	We took the bus.
1 Who did you stay with?		On Wednesday evening.
2 What did you visit while you were there?		At 11pm.
3 What time did you arrive at the airport?	→	Because I love Italian food.
4 How did you get there?		Some wonderful fish.
5 When did you come back?		With Marco's cousins.
6 What did you eat there?		The Tower of Pisa.

 29.6 LEE LA POSTAL Y RESPONDE A LAS PREGUNTAS

Dear Kim,

Greetings from London. We arrived on Wednesday, and then we went straight to the London Eye. It's amazing! On Thursday we visited the Tower of London. I bought a T-shirt in the shop there. Then yesterday we took a boat on the Thames and went to Greenwich. In the evening we had fish and chips.

Phil

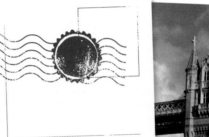

When did Phil arrive in London?	**Wednesday** ✓ **Thursday** ☐ **Friday** ☐
1 When did he go to the Tower of London?	**Wednesday** ☐ **Thursday** ☐ **Friday** ☐
2 What did Phil buy at the Tower of London?	**Tie** ☐ **A T-shirt** ☐ **A poster** ☐
3 How did Phil travel to Greenwich?	**By taxi** ☐ **By bus** ☐ **By boat** ☐
4 What did Phil eat in Greenwich?	**A burger** ☐ **Pizza** ☐ **Fish and chips** ☐

29.7 VUELVE A ESCRIBIR LAS FRASES PONIENDO LAS PALABRAS EN SU ORDEN CORRECTO

did | Why | you | Brazil? | go to

Why did you go to Brazil?

① you | When | did | Hong Kong? | visit

_____

② travel | with? | Who | you | did

_____

③ you | did | evening? | What | eat | in the

_____

④ buy | did | What | there? | you

_____

⑤ How | to | get | the | airport? | you | did

_____

⑥ visit | What | did | Rome? | in | you

_____

⑦ do | What | you | did | Las Vegas? | in

_____

29.8 DI LAS FRASES EN VOZ ALTA, CORRIGIENDO LOS ERRORES

What ____*did you do*____ on vacation?

We went walking in the mountains.

① Where _____ on vacation?

We went to France.

② When _____ at the hotel?

At about 9pm.

③ Who _____ on vacation with?

I went with my sister.

④ How _____ to the airport?

We took a taxi.

⑤ Why _____ to Sardinia?

Because it's a beautiful island.

⑥ What _____ at the restaurant?

We had fish and chips.

⑦ What _____ in Mallorca?

We went to some beautiful beaches.

30 Buscar trabajo

Si quieres encontrar empleo, debes conocer las palabras y expresiones en inglés que aparecen en los anuncios de trabajo y en las páginas web de las agencias de empleo.

⚙ **Lenguaje** Entrevistas de trabajo
Aa Vocabulario Expresiones sobre el trabajo
🧩 **Habilidad** Solicitar un empleo

30.1 LEE LAS OFERTAS DE EMPLEO Y RESPONDE A LAS PREGUNTAS

The job at Whiskers Animal Center is part time.
True ☐ **False** ☑

❶ No experience is needed for the job as a vet.
True ☐ **False** ☐

❷ The job at Brown Law Firm is on Thursdays.
True ☐ **False** ☐

❸ The job at Brown Law Firm is part-time.
True ☐ **False** ☐

❹ The waiter job is at lunchtimes.
True ☐ **False** ☐

❺ You need some experience for the waiter job.
True ☐ **False** ☐

---

52 BUSINESS TODAY

JOBS

WANTED
Vet at Whiskers Animal Centre, full time. Do you have a passion for animals? We need a vet to join our team. Two years' experience needed. £30,000 a year.

WANTED
Receptionist at Brown Law Firm, part-time. Are you friendly and outgoing? Do you work well in a team? We need a receptionist to work on Fridays and Saturdays (8am to 4pm), £10 an hour.

WANTED
Waiter at Alfredo's Pizzeria, evenings. We're looking for a hardworking waiter. Experience needed. Tuesday to Saturday (5pm to 11:30pm).

30.2 ESCUCHA EL AUDIO Y NUMERA LAS PREGUNTAS EN EL ORDEN EN QUE LAS ESCUCHES

Estas son algunas preguntas que te pueden hacer en una entrevista de trabajo.

🅐 Why did you study English in college? ☐

🅑 Why would you like this job? ☐

🅒 What experience do you have? ☐ 1

🅓 What do you like doing in your free time? ☐

🅔 When can you start work? ☐

🅕 Did you enjoy your time at chef school? ☐

🅖 Why did you leave your last job? ☐

🅗 Do you like working with people? ☐

30.3 LEE LA CARTA DE PRESENTACIÓN DE GARY Y COMPLETA LOS ESPACIOS EN LA DESCRIPCIÓN DE SU TRAYECTORIA LABORAL

Gary ___would like___ to apply for a job at LinguaPlus.

❶ He _____ an English teacher for two years.

❷ He _____ English in college.

❸ While _____ a student, he worked in a bar.

❹ He _____ working with others.

❺ Gary _____ English at St. Mark's School.

❻ He _____ at BKS Language Services.

❼ He _____ adults English now.

❽ He _____ soccer in his free time.

❾ He also _____ walking in the mountains.

Dear Mrs. O'Hanlon,

I would like to apply for the position of English teacher at LinguaPlus language school. I have been an English teacher for two years.
I studied English at Southern College. While I was a student I worked at Marco's Bar. I really liked working with other people.
After university, I worked at St. Mark's School, where I taught English. I am now working at BKS Language Services, where I teach adults English.
In my free time I love playing soccer and walking in the mountains.
I look forward to hearing from you soon.
Gary Smith

30.4 DI LAS PREGUNTAS EN VOZ ALTA, COMPLETANDO LOS ESPACIOS

What _____ _did you study_ _____ (study) at Manchester University?

❶ What _____ (do) at your last job at the restaurant?

❷ When _____ (start) working for our college?

❸ Why _____ (want) to work for our company?

❹ Where _____ (see) yourself in five years' time?

❺ _____ (like) working with other people?

❻ Why _____ (leave) your last job as a receptionist?

31 Tipos de preguntas

Existen dos tipos de preguntas: las preguntas de sujeto y las preguntas de objeto. Cada una se construye de forma diferente y sirven para preguntar cosas distintas.

☼ **Lenguaje** Preguntas de sujeto y de objeto
Aa Vocabulario El lugar de trabajo
Habilidad Hacer diferentes tipos de preguntas

31.1 ESCRIBE UNA PREGUNTA DE OBJETO PARA CADA AFIRMACIÓN

I had lunch with my boss on Monday.
Who *did you have lunch with on Monday?*

❶ I ate steak and salad for lunch.

What _____

❷ I went to the new café with John.

Who _____

❸ I saw a good presentation last week.

What _____

❹ Anna called Kim yesterday.

Who _____

❺ I visited a new customer on Wednesday.

Who _____

❻ David wants a job with a higher salary.

What _____

❼ Fiona likes having a nine-to-five job.

What _____

❽ I saw the new boss this morning.

Who _____

❾ Tina enjoys her job at the bank.

What _____

🔊

31.2 UTILIZA EL DIAGRAMA PARA CREAR 18 FRASES CORRECTAS Y DILAS EN VOZ ALTA

Who did you call yesterday?

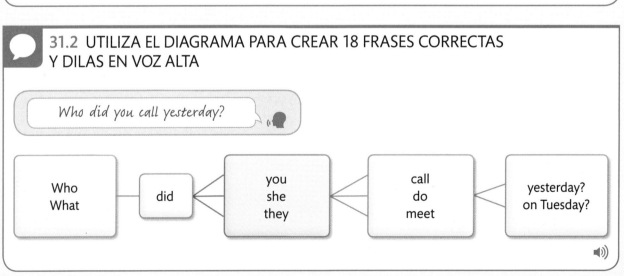

🔊

96

31.3 VUELVE A ESCRIBIR LAS FRASES PONIENDO LAS PALABRAS EN SU ORDEN CORRECTO

| this | sent | last | week? | Who | letter |

Who sent this letter last week?

1 | yesterday? | bank | called | the | Who |

_____

2 | new | did | order? | the | What | customer |

_____

3 | raise? | the | gave | a | Who | staff |

_____

4 | the | did | at | Who | meeting? | see | you |

_____

5 | the | does | want? | manager | What |

_____

6 | salary? | wants | Who | higher | a |

_____

7 | the | you? | say | What | boss | to | did |

_____

8 | call | on | Who | you | Monday? | did |

_____

9 | meeting | start? | What | time | the | did |

_____

31.4 REESCRIBE LAS FRASES COMO PREGUNTAS DE SUJETO

His old manager paid him a higher salary.
Who *paid him a higher salary?*

1 Stella emailed the prices to the customer.
Who _____

2 Harry started a full-time job last month.
Who _____

3 Paul doesn't want a nine-to-five job.
Who _____

4 The manager gave a presentation about sales.
Who _____

5 Alex and Joe had a good meeting yesterday.
Who _____

6 John didn't come to the meeting this morning.
Who _____

7 Dan started work at 7am today.
Who _____

8 Maria won the prize for Manager of the Month.
Who _____

9 The new office is big enough for the staff.
What _____

10 Jack wants to work for your company.
Who _____

11 The office party was great this year.
What _____

12 The new customer wants a discount.
Who _____

31.5 COMPLETA LOS ESPACIOS CON "WHO" O "WHAT" PARA ACABAR LAS PREGUNTAS

_____Who_____ bought a new laptop?

1 _____ asked for a higher salary?

2 _____ did Phil give the staff?

3 _____ gave a presentation?

4 _____ did she cook today?

5 _____ kind of job do you have?

6 _____ started a new job today?

7 _____ did you buy for Carla?

8 _____ didn't hit his sales targets?

9 _____ does she work for?

10 _____ sent the boss an email?

11 _____ did they say yesterday?

12 _____ did she meet on Tuesday?

13 _____ did you tell Amanda?

14 _____ asked for a discount?

15 _____ spoke to the customer?

16 _____ kind of music do you like?

17 _____ has a part-time job?

18 _____ gave the staff a day off?

19 _____ did Dan send the boss?

🔊

31.6 ESCUCHA EL AUDIO Y RESPONDE A LAS PREGUNTAS

Carlos le cuenta a Sarah un encuentro que tuvo en un restaurante.

When did Carlos go to the new restaurant?
Wednesday ☐   Friday ☑   Thursday ☐

1 Who did Carlos have lunch with last week?
his boss ☐   his brother ☐   his friend ☐

2 Did they like the food?
yes ☐   no ☐   they didn't order any ☐

3 Who had the special pizza?
Carlos ☐   his boss ☐   both of them ☐

4 Where is Carlos' new customer from?
Australia ☐   Canada ☐   the US ☐

5 What does his new customer's company make?
IT hardware ☐   IT software ☐   both ☐

6 Who does Carlos' new customer want to sell to?
the US ☐   Canada ☐   the UK ☐

7 How much is the bonus Carlos is getting?
£100 ☐   £300 ☐   £500 ☐

8 What other reward might Carlos get?
a promotion ☐   a holiday ☐   a raise ☐

9 Who does Sarah want to take to the restaurant?
Carlos ☐   Carlos' boss ☐   her boss ☐

31.7 MARCA LAS PREGUNTAS CORRECTAS

Who did give you the present? ☐
Who gave you the present? ☑

1 Who wrote to the customers? ☐
Who did write to the customers? ☐

2 Who met their sales targets this month? ☐
Who meet their sales targets this month? ☐

3 What asked the customer for? ☐
What did the customer ask for? ☐

4 Who did give a presentation? ☐
Who gave a presentation? ☐

5 What did the manager give the staff? ☐
What gave the manager the staff? ☐

6 Who called the new customers? ☐
Who did call the new customers? ☐

7 What ordered the new customer? ☐
What did the new customer order? ☐

8 What job did Sandra start last week? ☐
What job started Sandra last week? ☐

9 What time started the meeting? ☐
What time did the meeting start? ☐

10 Who did take notes at the meeting? ☐
Who took notes at the meeting? ☐

11 What did the area manager want? ☐
What wanted the area manager? ☐

12 Who wants a higher salary? ☐
Who does want a higher salary? ☐

13 What said the boss to you yesterday? ☐
What did the boss say to you yesterday? ☐

14 Who did call on Monday? ☐
Who called you on Monday? ☐

15 Who gave you the notes from the meeting? ☐
Who give you the notes from the meeting? ☐

16 What kind of job does Karen have? ☐
What kind of job has Karen? ☐

17 Who did you see at the meeting? ☐
Who did you saw at the meeting? ☐

◀))

31.8 UTILIZA EL DIAGRAMA PARA CREAR SEIS FRASES CORRECTAS Y DILAS EN VOZ ALTA

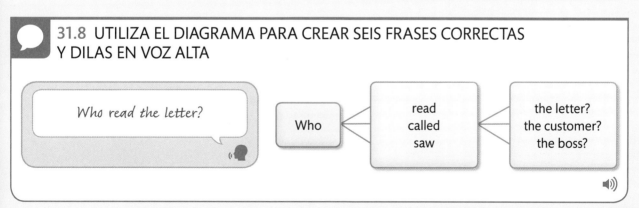

Who read the letter?

Who	read	the letter?
	called	the customer?
	saw	the boss?

◀))

32 "Someone", "anyone", "everyone"

Usa los pronombres indefinidos, como "anyone", "someone" o "everyone" para hacer referencia a una persona o a un grupo de personas sin especificar quiénes son.

⚙ **Lenguaje** Pronombres indefinidos
Aa Vocabulario La oficina
Habilidad Hablar de personas en general

 32.1 TACHA LA PALABRA INCORRECTA DE CADA FRASE

 I didn't see **anyone** / ~~someone~~ from school at the party on Saturday.

❶ There's **anyone** / someone at the door. Perhaps it's the new neighbor.

❷ My cousin wants **anyone** / someone to go on vacation with him to Argentina.

❸ I need **anyone** / someone to help me with my homework. It's very difficult.

❹ Does **anyone** / someone know John's phone number so I can give it to Sue?

❺ I met **anyone** / someone interesting on vacation and we went to the beach together.

❻ There's **anyone** / someone in the museum who you can ask for directions.

❼ Is **anyone** / someone going to see the movie tonight with Rachel and Monica?

❽ **Anyone** / Someone left an umbrella in the office on Monday.

❾ I need **anyone** / someone to go to the party with me tonight.

❿ Does **anyone** / someone want to go for coffee later in the café?

⓫ **Anyone** / Someone knocked on the door this morning when I was in the kitchen.

🔊

32.2 ESCUCHA EL AUDIO Y RESPONDE A LAS PREGUNTAS

Who went to the dance?
no one ☐ everyone ☐ someone ☑

1 Who wants some ice cream?
no one ☐ everyone ☐ someone ☐

2 Who saw the movie last night?
no one ☐ everyone ☐ someone ☐

3 Who is going abroad in the summer?
no one ☐ everyone ☐ someone ☐

4 Who wants to go to lunch with Sharon?
no one ☐ everyone ☐ someone ☐

5 Who likes the new boss?
no one ☐ everyone ☐ someone ☐

6 Who wants to go to a restaurant after work?
no one ☐ everyone ☐ someone ☐

7 Who will lend Kate a pencil?
no one ☐ everyone ☐ someone ☐

8 Who is going to the meeting later?
no one ☐ everyone ☐ someone ☐

32.3 REESCRIBE LAS FRASES CORRIGIENDO LOS ERRORES

Everybody **hate** our new office.
Everybody hates our new office.

1 I didn't give **nobody** your phone number.

_____

2 Is **somebody** coming for lunch with me?

_____

3 Nobody **like** my new green shirt.

_____

4 No one **are** coming to the movies tonight.

_____

5 **Anybody** remembered Ben's birthday. Poor Ben!

_____

6 Everyone **are** coming to my party tonight.

_____

7 Does **somebody** need help with the exercise?

_____

32.4 UTILIZA EL DIAGRAMA PARA CREAR NUEVE FRASES CORRECTAS Y DILAS EN VOZ ALTA

Everybody went to the restaurant last night.

| Everybody Someone Nobody | went to asked wants | the restaurant last night. about the new job. to go to a party with me tonight. |

33 Mantener una conversación

Las preguntas cortas son una manera de mostrar tu interés mientras hablas con alguien. Puedes utilizarlas para mantener la conversación activa.

🎛 **Lenguaje** Preguntas cortas
Aa Vocabulario Palabras de pregunta
🏃 **Habilidad** Hacer preguntas cortas

33.1 MARCA LA PREGUNTA CORTA DE CADA AFIRMACIÓN

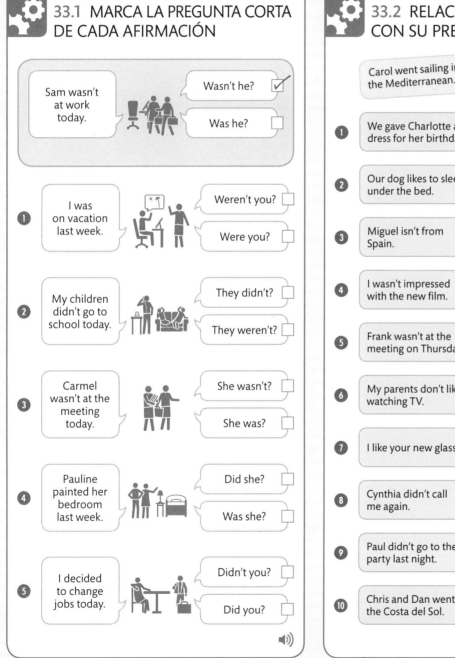

Sam wasn't at work today.
Wasn't he? ✓
Was he?

1 I was on vacation last week.
Weren't you?
Were you?

2 My children didn't go to school today.
They didn't?
They weren't?

3 Carmel wasn't at the meeting today.
She wasn't?
She was?

4 Pauline painted her bedroom last week.
Did she?
Was she?

5 I decided to change jobs today.
Didn't you?
Did you?

33.2 RELACIONA CADA FRASE CON SU PREGUNTA CORTA

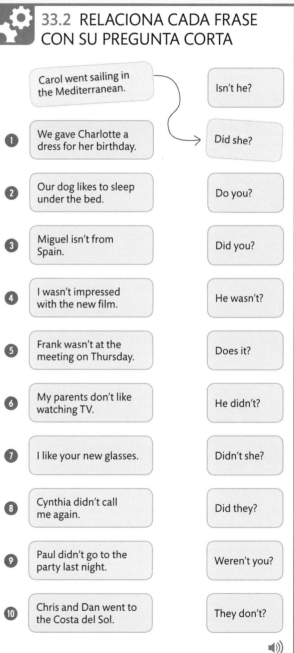

Carol went sailing in the Mediterranean.
Isn't he?

1 We gave Charlotte a dress for her birthday.
Did she?

2 Our dog likes to sleep under the bed.
Do you?

3 Miguel isn't from Spain.
Did you?

4 I wasn't impressed with the new film.
He wasn't?

5 Frank wasn't at the meeting on Thursday.
Does it?

6 My parents don't like watching TV.
He didn't?

7 I like your new glasses.
Didn't she?

8 Cynthia didn't call me again.
Did they?

9 Paul didn't go to the party last night.
Weren't you?

10 Chris and Dan went to the Costa del Sol.
They don't?

33.3 COMPLETA LAS PREGUNTAS CORTAS EN FUNCIÓN DE LAS FRASES

I really want to see the new movie.
_____*Do*_____ you?

❶ Maria likes listening to opera.

_____ she?

❷ Phillip went to Greece on vacation.

He _____ ?

❸ Greg comes from Australia.

_____ he?

❹ I don't have a car.

You _____ ?

❺ My children hate reading books.

They _____ ?

❻ Shelly isn't at home right now.

_____ she?

❼ Kim wasn't at the party last night.

_____ she?

33.4 RESPONDE AL AUDIO EN VOZ ALTA

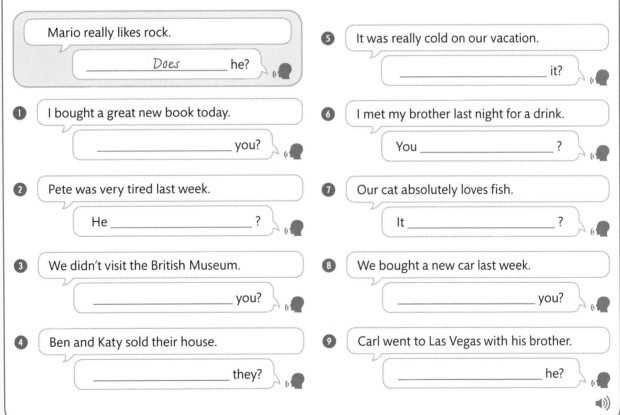

Mario really likes rock.

_____*Does*_____ he?

❶ I bought a great new book today.

_____ you?

❷ Pete was very tired last week.

He _____ ?

❸ We didn't visit the British Museum.

_____ you?

❹ Ben and Katy sold their house.

_____ they?

❺ It was really cold on our vacation.

_____ it?

❻ I met my brother last night for a drink.

You _____ ?

❼ Our cat absolutely loves fish.

It _____ ?

❽ We bought a new car last week.

_____ you?

❾ Carl went to Las Vegas with his brother.

_____ he?

34 Vocabulario

Aa 34.1 SALIR ESCRIBE LAS PALABRAS DEL RECUADRO BAJO SU IMAGEN

show

1 _____

2 _____

3 _____

4 _____

5 _____

7 _____

8 _____

9 _____

10 _____

11 _____

14 _____

15 _____

16 _____

17 _____

18 _____

21 _____

22 _____

23 _____

24 _____

25 _____

5 _____

6 _____

12 _____

13 _____

19 _____

20 _____

26 _____

27 _____

art gallery   bar   go bowling

buy a ticket   fun fair   opera

~~show~~   go dancing

circus   musician   orchestra

meet friends   waitress

menu   night club   audience

restaurant   see a play

concert hall   applause   waiter

book club   concert

do karaoke   ballet   go to a party

band   go to the movies

35 Planes futuros

Puedes utilizar el present continuous para hablar de cosas que están ocurriendo ahora. También sirve para hablar de planes futuros.

⚙️ **Lenguaje** El futuro con present continuous
Aa Vocabulario Excusas
🧩 **Habilidad** Hablar de planes futuros

35.1 COMPLETA LOS ESPACIOS PONIENDO LOS VERBOS EN PRESENT CONTINUOUS

Terry _____*is visiting*_____ (🧍 visit) his grandparents this weekend.

1 We _____ (⛵ go) sailing in the Mediterranean this summer.

2 Shelley _____ (🧍 travel) around India in July next year.

3 We _____ (🏃 play) baseball with our friends after school.

4 I _____ (👥 watch) a movie at the theater with my boyfriend tonight.

🔊

35.2 LEE EL CORREO Y MARCA SI LAS FRASES SE REFIEREN AL PRESENTE O AL FUTURO

✉️ ⌄ ✕

To: Carol

Subject: Plan for the week

Hi Carol,
Thanks for inviting me to dinner next week. I'm very busy at the moment, because I'm writing a book. But I'll tell you my plan for the week. On Monday and Tuesday, I'm playing tennis with Cathy. Cathy is living in London now. On Wednesday, I'm visiting Mike. Mike is working at the school on Grange Road. He really loves it there. On Thursday, I'm going swimming with Paula. It'll be great to see her.
Susan

↩ ↩↩   📎 🗑

Susan is writing a book.
Presente ✓   **Futuro** ☐

1 Susan is playing tennis with Cathy.
Presente ☐   **Futuro** ☐

2 Cathy is living in London.
Presente ☐   **Futuro** ☐

3 Mike is working at the school.
Presente ☐   **Futuro** ☐

4 Susan is going swimming with Paula.
Presente ☐   **Futuro** ☐

35.3 TACHA LA PALABRA INCORRECTA DE CADA FRASE

I'm graduating ~~on~~ / in 2016.

1. We're going to France on / in June.

2. I'm playing tennis on / in Wednesday.

3. My grandmother was born on / in 1944.

4. Christmas Day is on / in December 25.

5. I'm finishing work on / in 2025.

6. I bought a new car on / in Wednesday.

7. New Year's Day is on / in January 1.

8. Pete was born on / in 1990.

9. I saw my friend Clive on / in Saturday.

10. Derek starts his job on / in Tuesday.

11. Alexander's exam is on / in June 4.

12. We finish school on / in July.

13. I'm going to the theater on / in Friday evening.

35.4 RESPONDE AL AUDIO EN VOZ ALTA Y COLOCA LOS VERBOS DEL RECUADRO EN PRESENT CONTINUOUS

Would you like to go swimming this weekend?

Sorry, I can't. I _____ *am visiting* _____ my grandmother.

1. Do you want to go to the movies tomorrow?

   I'd love to, but I can't. I _____ for my exam.

2. Would you like to go to Franco's restaurant tonight?

   That would be nice, but I _____ my girlfriend in town.

3. Would you like to play golf with me next week?

   Oh, I'd love to, but I _____ on vacation to Spain.

4. Would you like to have lunch with us today?

   I'd like to, but I can't. I _____ lunch with Sue today.

| have | study | go | meet | ~~visit~~ |

35.5 LEE EL CORREO Y RESPONDE A LAS PREGUNTAS

To: Paul

Subject: Travel plans

Hi Paul,

Thanks for the invite! I'd love to come with you to Italy, but I'm traveling to Greece in June. But I'm coming to Paris in July, so hopefully we can meet then. I have some news. My granddad is retiring. So, we are having a party in August. All the family is coming. I hope you'll be there. I'm having a really busy week. I'm studying for my exams at the moment. I have a big English exam on May 7. Then, on Tuesday, I'm playing golf. It's a big competition, and I hope I'm going to win. Aside from that, I'm going to the theater with Emma tonight.

How are things with you?

Tony

Tony is traveling to Greece in July.

True ☐ **False** ☑

❶ Tony is coming to Paris in July.

True ☐ **False** ☐

❷ Tony's grandmother is retiring in August.

True ☐ **False** ☐

❸ Tony is studying for his English exam.

True ☐ **False** ☐

❹ Tony's exam is on May 8.

True ☐ **False** ☐

❺ Tony is playing tennis on Tuesday.

True ☐ **False** ☐

35.6 ESCUCHA EL AUDIO Y UNE LOS NOMBRES CON LAS EXCUSAS

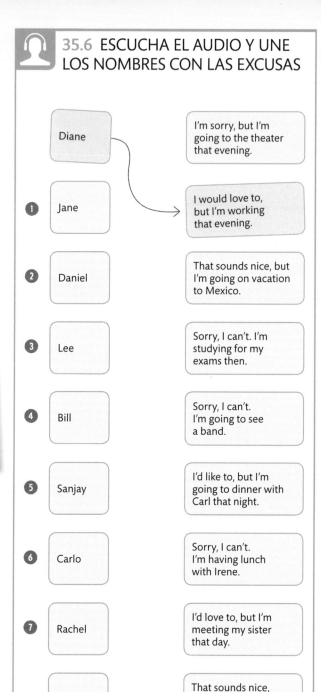

Diane — I'm sorry, but I'm going to the theater that evening.

❶ Jane → I would love to, but I'm working that evening.

❷ Daniel — That sounds nice, but I'm going on vacation to Mexico.

❸ Lee — Sorry, I can't. I'm studying for my exams then.

❹ Bill — Sorry, I can't. I'm going to see a band.

❺ Sanjay — I'd like to, but I'm going to dinner with Carl that night.

❻ Carlo — Sorry, I can't. I'm having lunch with Irene.

❼ Rachel — I'd love to, but I'm meeting my sister that day.

❽ May — That sounds nice, but I'm going shopping with Tom.

❾ Sarah — I'd love to, but I'm playing soccer with my colleagues.

35.7 LEE LA AGENDA Y RESPONDE A LAS PREGUNTAS EN VOZ ALTA

September

MONDAY 5	Go swimming
TUESDAY 6	Go to the movies
WEDNESDAY 7	Visit old friends from school
THURSDAY 8	Study for the math exam
FRIDAY 9	Go to Sam's party
SATURDAY 10	Visit my grandparents
SUNDAY 11	Go ice skating with Victoria
MONDAY 12	Shop for groceries

Would you like to come to dinner on Tuesday?

I would love to, but _I am going to the movies_ .

4 Would you like to play soccer on Friday?

That would be fun, but _____ _____ .

1 Do you want to play soccer on Sunday?

That'd be fun, but _____ _____ .

5 Do you want to go to a party on Saturday?

Sorry I can't. _____ _____ .

2 Would you like to go to a café on Monday?

I'd like to, but _____ _____ .

6 Would you like to go ice skating on Thursday?

That sounds nice, but _____ _____ .

3 Would you like to go running on Wednesday?

That sounds nice, but _____ _____ .

7 Do you want to go out for lunch next Monday?

I can't. _____ _____ .

36 Planes e intenciones

Puedes utilizar "going to" para hablar de lo que quieres hacer en un futuro. También sirve para hablar de planes específicos, para hablar de cuándo y dónde vas a hacer algo.

⚙ **Lenguaje** Tiempos verbales de futuro
Aa Vocabulario Palabras y expresiones temporales
🦶 **Habilidad** Hablar de tus planes

36.1 LEE EL CORREO Y RESPONDE A LAS PREGUNTAS

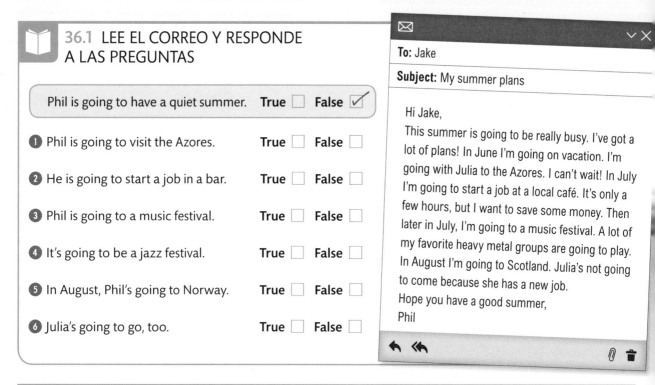

✉	⌄ ✕
To: Jake	
Subject: My summer plans	

Hi Jake,

This summer is going to be really busy. I've got a lot of plans! In June I'm going on vacation. I'm going with Julia to the Azores. I can't wait! In July I'm going to start a job at a local café. It's only a few hours, but I want to save some money. Then later in July, I'm going to a music festival. A lot of my favorite heavy metal groups are going to play. In August I'm going to Scotland. Julia's not going to come because she has a new job.
Hope you have a good summer,
Phil

> Phil is going to have a quiet summer.　**True** ☐　**False** ☑

1 Phil is going to visit the Azores.　**True** ☐　**False** ☐

2 He is going to start a job in a bar.　**True** ☐　**False** ☐

3 Phil is going to a music festival.　**True** ☐　**False** ☐

4 It's going to be a jazz festival.　**True** ☐　**False** ☐

5 In August, Phil's going to Norway.　**True** ☐　**False** ☐

6 Julia's going to go, too.　**True** ☐　**False** ☐

36.2 TACHA LAS PALABRAS INCORRECTAS DE CADA FRASE

> I ~~is~~ / ~~are~~ / am going start a new language course.

1 Angela is / are / am going to clean her bedroom.

2 Will is / are / am not going to buy a new car.

3 They is / are / am going to stay in a hotel.

4 Mary and George is / are / am going to visit Egypt.

5 Shane is / are / am going to study IT in college.

6 You is / are / am going to visit your grandmother.

7 Liv is / are / am going to finish her work later.

8 Aziz is / are / am going to travel to Rome this fall.

9 They is / are / am not going to play soccer today.

10 I is / are / am going to cook steak tonight.

11 We is / are / am going to eat pizza for dinner.

12 Murat is / are / am going to listen to the radio.

13 I is / are / am not going to eat frogs' legs again.

🔊

36.3 VUELVE A ESCRIBIR LAS FRASES PONIENDO LAS PALABRAS EN SU ORDEN CORRECTO

is to Karen going her house. paint

Karen is going to paint her house.

1 to pizza Tim eat tonight. is going

_____

2 not is drive to Ann to going Utah.

_____

3 Boston going are this to fall. We visit

_____

4 going Fred is to German. study not

_____

5 buy are going They to a puppy.

_____

6 I to this am travel going summer.

_____

7 soccer. play are going to We

_____

8 going I'm start to an English course.

_____

9 is to her clean going room. Angela

_____

10 going I to at study the library. am

_____

11 their to going They are sell house.

_____

◀))

36.4 COMPLETA LOS ESPACIOS UTILIZANDO VERBOS EN FUTURO CON "GOING TO"

Chris and Sam _____*are going to watch*_____ (watch) a movie tonight.

1 We _____ (cook) a chicken tonight.

2 Sharon and Flo _____ (not play) tennis this weekend.

3 I _____ (visit) my aunt in France in September.

4 Pedro _____ (learn) a musical instrument at school.

◀))

111

Aa 36.5 CONECTA LOS DIBUJOS CON SUS DESCRIPCIONES

Janet is going to visit Hawaii.

Tim is going to climb a mountain.

Sharon is going to bake a cake.

Cynthia is going to walk her dog.

Mike is going to watch a movie.

Phil is going to take a photo.

💬 36.6 DI LAS FRASES EN VOZ ALTA, COMPLETANDO LOS ESPACIOS

You _are going to watch_ (watch) a movie this evening.

1. I _____ (visit) Berlin next week.

2. Rachel _____ (paint) her kitchen on the weekend.

3. My sister _____ (study) French in college.

4. Stuart and Colin _____ (climb) that mountain.

5. Patrick _____ (not drive) to work today.

6. Angus _____ (live) in Edinburgh.

7. We _____ (buy) a new house.

8. Samantha _____ (watch) a movie tonight.

9. Helen _____ (start) her new job next week.

36.7 CONECTA EL INICIO Y EL FINAL DE CADA FRASE

Tom is going to save	a cake for Christmas.
① Jessica is not going to study	for his job interview.
② We are going to paint	a hamburger for lunch.
③ Jenny is going to go	enough money by Christmas.
④ Theo is going to wear a suit	the kitchen a different color.
⑤ My uncle is not going to eat	her horse this weekend.
⑥ Olivia is going to ride	physics in college.
⑦ I am going to bake	on vacation in the Bahamas.

36.8 ESCUCHA EL AUDIO Y NUMERA LAS IMÁGENES EN EL ORDEN EN QUE SE DESCRIBEN

37 Lo que va a ocurrir

Utiliza el futuro con "going to" para hacer una predicción sobre el futuro cuando tengas alguna pista en el presente que respalde dicha prediccion.

⚙ **Lenguaje** El futuro con "going to"
Aa Vocabulario Verbos de predicción
🧩 **Habilidad** Predecir acontecimientos futuros

Aa 37.1 OBSERVA LOS DIBUJOS Y COMPLETA LOS ESPACIOS CON LAS PALABRAS DEL RECUADRO

He's going to ___*sing*___ a song.

❶ The boy is going to _____ the wall.

❷ It looks like it's going to _____ soon.

❸ It's 8:29pm. We're going to _____ the train.

❹ Oh dear! I think they're going to _____.

❺ I think she's going to _____ that coat.

| fall off | crash | buy | rain | miss | ~~sing~~ |

🔊

114

37.2 VUELVE A ESCRIBIR LAS FRASES CORRIGIENDO LOS ERRORES

> Jenny has finished all her final exams. She are going to leave school soon.
> *Jenny has finished all her final exams. She is going to leave school soon.*

1 Oh no, it's started to rain cats and dogs. We going to get wet!

_____

2 That girl has been teasing the dog all day. I think it is going bite her.

_____

3 Hurry up! The train leaves in five minutes and you is going to miss it.

_____

4 That's Claire's purse. She's going leave for college in a minute.

_____

5 It looks like he going to win this race. He's a long way in front.

_____

6 The team captain has a microphone. Do you think he's going sing the national anthem?

_____

7 The weather forecast says it are not going to rain at all next week.

_____

8 This traffic jam is enormous. I is going to be late for work again.

_____

9 That dog is trying to open your shopping bag. I think he's go to steal your food.

_____

10 Raymond are going to study science in college.

_____

11 Shelley not going to win the competition. The other players are all too good.

_____

12 They're not very good at skating. It looks like they is going to fall over.

_____

🔊

37.3 VUELVE A ESCRIBIR LAS FRASES PONIENDO LAS PALABRAS EN SU ORDEN CORRECTO

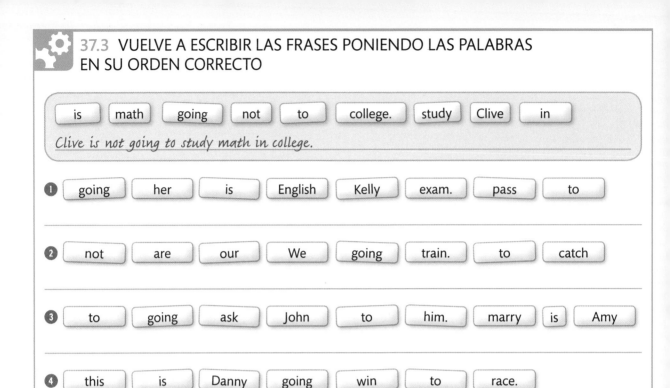

| is | math | going | not | to | college. | study | Clive | in |

Clive is not going to study math in college.

1 | going | her | is | English | Kelly | exam. | pass | to |

_____

2 | not | are | our | We | going | train. | to | catch |

_____

3 | to | going | ask | John | to | him. | marry | is | Amy |

_____

4 | this | is | Danny | going | win | to | race. |

_____

Aa 37.4 CONECTA EL INICIO Y EL FINAL DE CADA FRASE

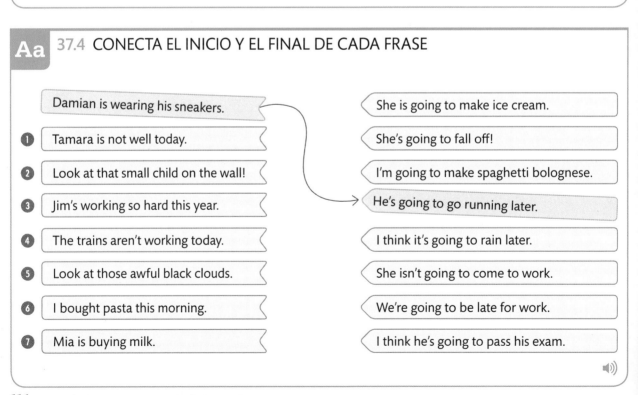

Damian is wearing his sneakers. ——→ He's going to go running later.

1 Tamara is not well today.

2 Look at that small child on the wall!

3 Jim's working so hard this year.

4 The trains aren't working today.

5 Look at those awful black clouds.

6 I bought pasta this morning.

7 Mia is buying milk.

She is going to make ice cream.

She's going to fall off!

I'm going to make spaghetti bolognese.

He's going to go running later.

I think it's going to rain later.

She isn't going to come to work.

We're going to be late for work.

I think he's going to pass his exam.

37.5 COMPLETA LOS ESPACIOS CON LOS VERBOS EN FORMA FUTURA CON "GOING TO"

Charmaine _____*is going to send*_____ (send) a letter.

❶ Sharon _____ (eat) a piece of cake.

❷ Take an umbrella. It _____ (rain) later.

❸ The children _____ (enjoy) the movie tonight.

❹ My husband _____ (be) late for work.

❺ Mrs. O'Connell _____ (play) the piano in a minute.

❻ Be careful! You _____ (drop) the vase.

❼ Bill and Claire _____ (bake) a birthday cake for Paul.

🔊

37.6 UTILIZA EL DIAGRAMA PARA CREAR 18 FRASES CORRECTAS Y DILAS EN VOZ ALTA

I am going to be late for work.

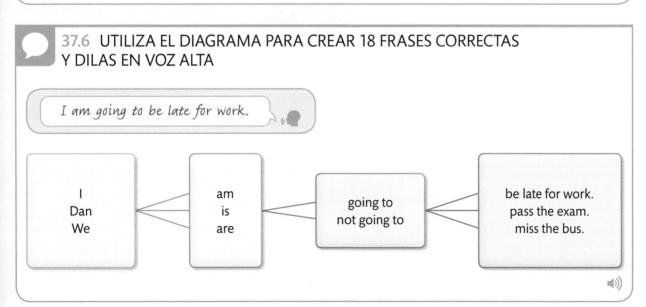

| I / Dan / We | am / is / are | going to / not going to | be late for work. / pass the exam. / miss the bus. |

🔊

117

38 Vocabulario

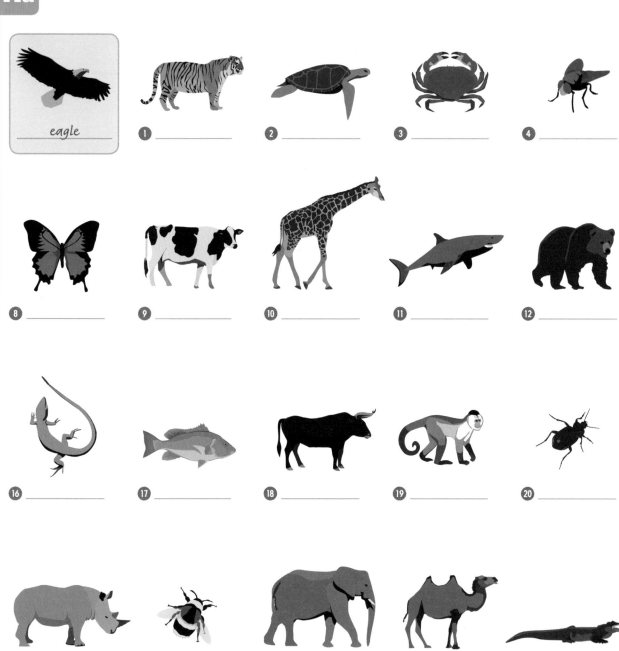

eagle

1 _____

2 _____

3 _____

4 _____

8 _____

9 _____

10 _____

11 _____

12 _____

16 _____

17 _____

18 _____

19 _____

20 _____

24 _____

25 _____

26 _____

27 _____

28 _____

5 _____

6 _____

7 _____

13 _____

14 _____

15 _____

21 _____

22 _____

23 _____

29 _____

30 _____

31 _____

lion	giraffe
rhino	bull
elephant	~~eagle~~
bee	dolphin
butterfly	snake
lizard	fish
octopus	cow
buffalo	monkey
spider	crab
shark	tiger

bird   rat   insect

fly   turtle   bear

crocodile	camel
whale	mouse
kangaroo	frog

39 Hacer predicciones

Puedes utilizar el verbo "will" para hablar de acontecimientos futuros en inglés. Esta forma de futuro tiene un significado un poco diferente de las formas futuras con "going to".

⚙ **Lenguaje** El futuro con "will"
Aa Vocabulario Palabras de predicción
🧩 **Habilidad** Decir lo que crees que pasará

⚙ **39.1 COMPLETA LOS ESPACIOS PONIENDO LOS VERBOS EN FUTURO CON "WILL"**

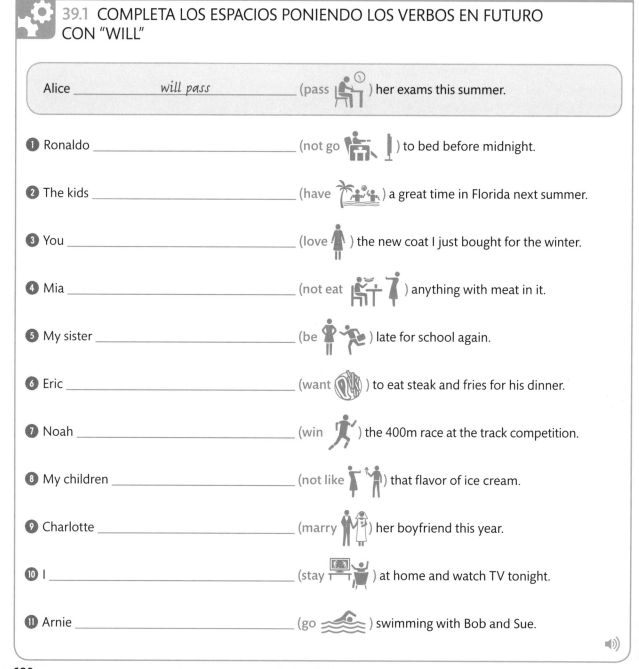

Alice _____*will pass*_____ (pass 🪑) her exams this summer.

1 Ronaldo _____ (not go 📺) to bed before midnight.

2 The kids _____ (have 🏖) a great time in Florida next summer.

3 You _____ (love 🧍) the new coat I just bought for the winter.

4 Mia _____ (not eat 🍽) anything with meat in it.

5 My sister _____ (be 🏃) late for school again.

6 Eric _____ (want 🍝) to eat steak and fries for his dinner.

7 Noah _____ (win 🏃) the 400m race at the track competition.

8 My children _____ (not like 🍦) that flavor of ice cream.

9 Charlotte _____ (marry 👰) her boyfriend this year.

10 I _____ (stay 📺) at home and watch TV tonight.

11 Arnie _____ (go 🏊) swimming with Bob and Sue.

🔊

39.2 VUELVE A ESCRIBIR LAS FRASES UTILIZANDO LAS FORMAS CORTAS DE "WILL" Y "WILL NOT"

We will go to the shops.	=	We'll go to the shops.

1 Chris will not go on vacation this year. = _____

2 I will write you a postcard from Ibiza. = _____

3 They will visit their grandmother next week. = _____

4 Ethan will not go to summer camp this year. = _____

5 Isla will not reply to my messages. = _____

6 We will visit you when we are in San Diego. = _____

7 I will not be at the party this evening. = _____

8 Eleanor will not make dinner for us tonight. = _____

9 I will take the children to the movie theater tonight. = _____

10 Fred will not be at the party tomorrow. = _____

39.3 VUELVE A ESCRIBIR LAS FRASES MARCADAS UTILIZANDO UN PRONOMBRE Y LA FORMA CONTRAÍDA DEL VERBO

She'll bring some salad.

1 _____

2 _____

3 _____

4 _____

5 _____

Hi Peter,

The picnic on Saturday is going to be fantastic. I can't wait. Is there anything you'd like me to bring? Chloe will bring some salad, she always makes one for us. David will bring some chicken and Sarah will make some sandwiches. I think Martha will get some juice. Hopefully Sharon and Andrew will make a cake. I just hope the weather will be nice and sunny! I can bring some salami and some cheese if you like.

See you Saturday,

Doug

39.4 VUELVE A ESCRIBIR LAS FRASES CON "I THINK" O "I DON'T THINK"

> It won't rain this afternoon.
> _I don't think it will rain this afternoon._

❶ I'll visit Rome next year.

_____

❷ Bob won't be at the party.

_____

❸ We'll go to a restaurant tonight.

_____

❹ My brother will visit us this year.

_____

❺ The kids won't go to school tomorrow.

_____

❻ It won't be sunny tomorrow.

_____

❼ We'll win the lottery this week.

_____

❽ Simone will want to go to the theater.

_____

❾ It won't snow this winter.

_____

 39.5 TACHA LAS PALABRAS INCORRECTAS DE CADA FRASE

NOTA
Utiliza "will" en predicciones para las que no tengas prueba, y "going to" en predicciones para las que cuentes con una prueba clara.

> I think you ~~are going to~~ / will really enjoy this book.

❶ Look at those clouds. It **is going to** / will rain.

❷ You **isn't going to** / won't like this movie.

❸ There's so much traffic! We **are going to** / will be late.

❹ Bob never does his homework. He **is going to** / will fail the exam.

❺ Will he / **Are he going to** come to the party tomorrow?

❻ Jenny practices the guitar every day. She **is going to** / will be a great musician.

❼ Bob looks tired. He **isn't going to** / won't finish the race.

❽ I think Chloe **is going to** / will not win the competition. I love her voice.

❾ Peter **is going to** / will fall asleep. He looks tired.

❿ It **is going to be** / will be a delicious meal.

39.6 LEE EL CORREO Y RESPONDE A LAS PREGUNTAS CON FRASES COMPLETAS

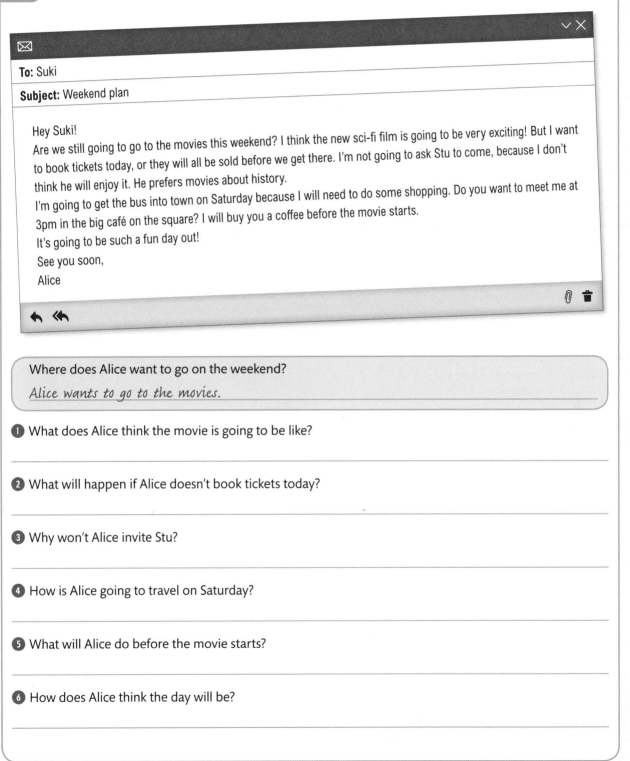

To: Suki

Subject: Weekend plan

Hey Suki!
Are we still going to go to the movies this weekend? I think the new sci-fi film is going to be very exciting! But I want to book tickets today, or they will all be sold before we get there. I'm not going to ask Stu to come, because I don't think he will enjoy it. He prefers movies about history.
I'm going to get the bus into town on Saturday because I will need to do some shopping. Do you want to meet me at 3pm in the big café on the square? I will buy you a coffee before the movie starts.
It's going to be such a fun day out!
See you soon,
Alice

Where does Alice want to go on the weekend?

Alice wants to go to the movies.

❶ What does Alice think the movie is going to be like?

_____

❷ What will happen if Alice doesn't book tickets today?

_____

❸ Why won't Alice invite Stu?

_____

❹ How is Alice going to travel on Saturday?

_____

❺ What will Alice do before the movie starts?

_____

❻ How does Alice think the day will be?

_____

40 Tomar decisiones rápidas

Puedes utilizar "will" para hablar del futuro de dos maneras: cuando haces una predicción sin pruebas, o cuando tomas una decisión rápida acerca de algo.

🔧 **Lenguaje** Decisiones rápidas con "will"
Aa Vocabulario Palabras de decisión
Habilidad Hablar de acciones futuras

40.1 COMPLETA LOS ESPACIOS PONIENDO LOS VERBOS EN FUTURO CON "WILL" Y "WON'T"

It's raining, so we ___*won't walk*___ (not walk). We ___*will go*___ (go) there by car.

1. There's no milk, so I _____ (not have) tea. I _____ (have) black coffee.

2. The 11:05 train is late, so we _____ (not get) that one. We _____ (take) the bus.

3. I don't feel well. I _____ (not go) to work. I _____ (call) my boss and tell him.

4. I left work late yesterday. I _____ (not stay) late today. I _____ (leave) at 5pm.

5. I'm tired. I _____ (not make) dinner. I _____ (ask) my partner to make it.

6. There are no buses and it's raining. I _____ (not walk) . I _____ (get) a taxi home.

7. It is snowing. I _____ (not drive) to work. I _____ (get) the bus today.

8. It's late. I _____ (not walk) the dog in the park. I _____ (walk) up the road instead.

9. It's sunny. I _____ (not take) an umbrella. I _____ (wear) my sun hat.

10. There's a lot of traffic. I _____ (not drive) . I _____ (walk) there.

11. I _____ (not take) my books back to the library. I _____ (do) it tomorrow.

40.2 ESCUCHA EL AUDIO Y MARCA SI LAS PERSONAS QUE HABLAN VAN A HACER O NO LAS ACTIVIDADES

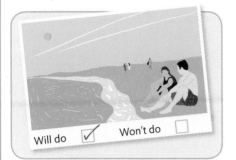

Will do ✓   Won't do ☐

❶ Will do ☐   Won't do ☐

❷ Will do ☐   Won't do ☐

❸ Will do ☐   Won't do ☐

❹ Will do ☐   Won't do ☐

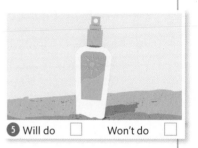

❺ Will do ☐   Won't do ☐

40.3 CONECTA EL INICIO Y EL FINAL DE CADA FRASE

There's too much traffic, so

❶ It's going to rain, so

❷ It's my sister's birthday today, so

❸ I forgot my sandwich, so

❹ I like those jeans, so

❺ It's dark, so

❻ It's a long train trip, so

❼ There's nothing to eat, so

I'll make her a cake.

I'll take a book with me.

I'll buy them.

I'll walk there.

I won't walk home through the park.

I'll take an umbrella with me.

I'll get a takeout pizza.

I'll buy one from the deli.

40.4 RESPONDE AL AUDIO EN VOZ ALTA UTILIZANDO LAS PALABRAS DEL RECUADRO

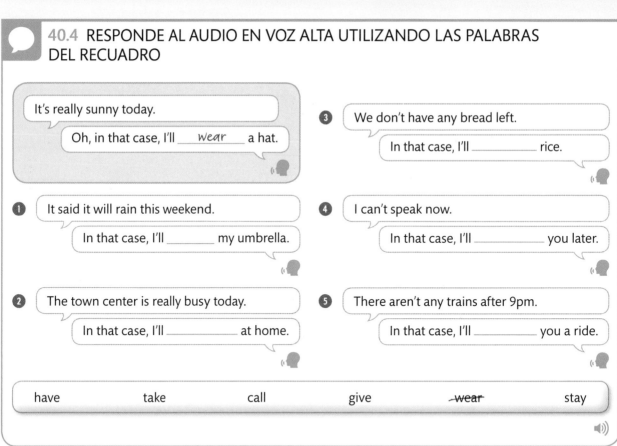

It's really sunny today.

Oh, in that case, I'll ___wear___ a hat.

1 It said it will rain this weekend.

In that case, I'll _____ my umbrella.

2 The town center is really busy today.

In that case, I'll _____ at home.

3 We don't have any bread left.

In that case, I'll _____ rice.

4 I can't speak now.

In that case, I'll _____ you later.

5 There aren't any trains after 9pm.

In that case, I'll _____ you a ride.

have	take	call	give	~~wear~~	stay

40.5 VUELVE A ESCRIBIR LAS FRASES PONIENDO LAS PALABRAS EN SU ORDEN CORRECTO

go | I'll | to | I | think | bed.
I think I'll go to bed.

1 I | have | I'll | fish. | think | the
_____

2 tonight. | I | stay | think | I'll | in
_____

3 think | watch | I | news. | I'll | the
_____

4 take | think | my | I'll | raincoat. | I
_____

5 Simon. | think | I | call | I'll
_____

6 leave | I | work | I'll | early. | think
_____

7 Jenny | to | I | dinner. | think | I'll | ask | make
_____

126

40.6 LEE EL CHAT Y RESPONDE A LAS PREGUNTAS

It's the English class party next Friday.
True ✓ False ☐

❶ Two students will decorate with balloons.
True ☐ False ☐

❷ John won't help Kate.
True ☐ False ☐

❸ Everyone will make a banner with their names on it.
True ☐ False ☐

❹ Harry will arrange the music for the party.
True ☐ False ☐

❺ Josie's band will definitely play at the party.
True ☐ False ☐

❻ Arthur will play in a band at the party.
True ☐ False ☐

❼ Janet will make two cakes.
True ☐ False ☐

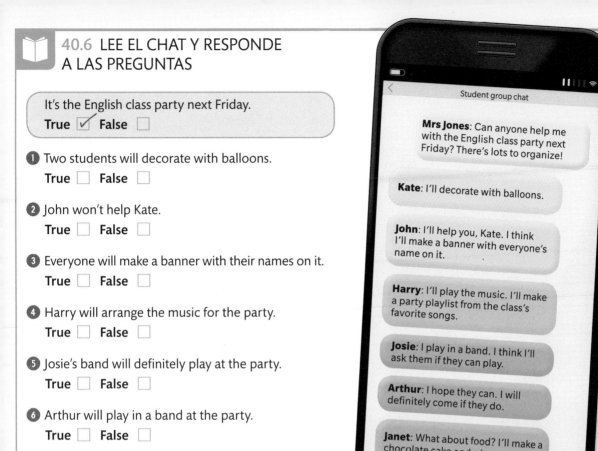

Student group chat

Mrs Jones: Can anyone help me with the English class party next Friday? There's lots to organize!

Kate: I'll decorate with balloons.

John: I'll help you, Kate. I think I'll make a banner with everyone's name on it.

Harry: I'll play the music. I'll make a party playlist from the class's favorite songs.

Josie: I play in a band. I think I'll ask them if they can play.

Arthur: I hope they can. I will definitely come if they do.

Janet: What about food? I'll make a chocolate cake and a lemon cake.

40.7 UTILIZA EL DIAGRAMA PARA CREAR 10 FRASES CORRECTAS Y DILAS EN VOZ ALTA

I think he'll win the race.

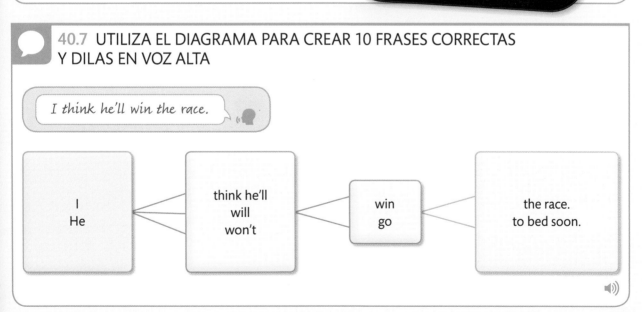

| I / He | think he'll / will / won't | win / go | the race. / to bed soon. |

41 Posibilidades futuras

Utiliza "might" para indicar que no estás seguro de si harás algo. Es una posibilidad y no quieres decir aún si vas a hacerlo ("will") o no ("won't").

⚙ **Lenguaje** Utilizar "might"

Aa Vocabulario Actividades, comida y aficiones

🏃 **Habilidad** Hablar de posibilidades futuras

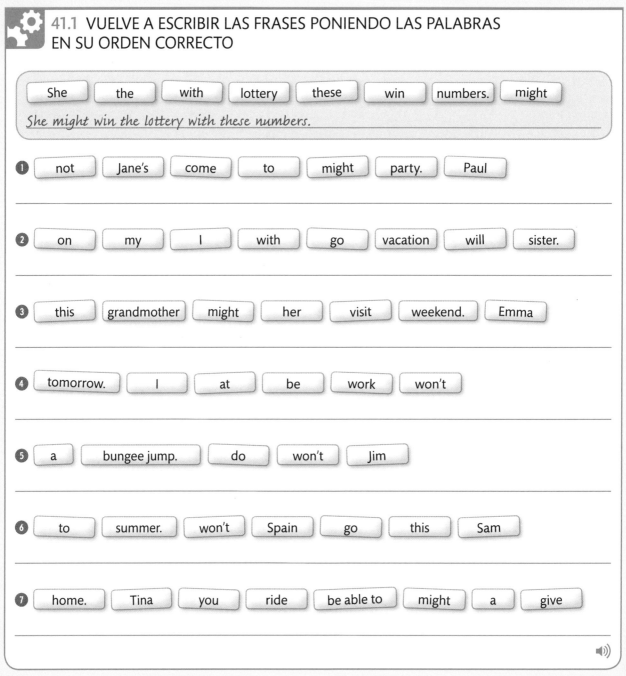

41.1 VUELVE A ESCRIBIR LAS FRASES PONIENDO LAS PALABRAS EN SU ORDEN CORRECTO

| She | the | with | lottery | these | win | numbers. | might |

She might win the lottery with these numbers.

1. | not | Jane's | come | to | might | party. | Paul |

_____

2. | on | my | I | with | go | vacation | will | sister. |

_____

3. | this | grandmother | might | her | visit | weekend. | Emma |

_____

4. | tomorrow. | I | at | be | work | won't |

_____

5. | a | bungee jump. | do | won't | Jim |

_____

6. | to | summer. | won't | Spain | go | this | Sam |

_____

7. | home. | Tina | you | ride | be able to | might | a | give |

_____

🔊

41.2 COMPLETA LOS ESPACIOS PARA ESCRIBIR CADA FRASE DE TRES MANERAS DISTINTAS

I won't buy a computer.	I might buy a computer.	I will buy a computer.
1 _____	I might go to the movies tonight.	_____
2 We won't go to Dan's party.	_____	_____
3 _____	_____	I will go to the bank at lunchtime.
4 _____	I might buy a newspaper.	_____
5 You won't work late tonight.	_____	_____
6 _____	_____	Karen will move next month.

41.3 VUELVE A ESCRIBIR LAS FRASES MARCADAS CORRIGIENDO LOS ERRORES

⌄ ✕

✉

To: Eric

Subject: Travel plans

Hi Eric,

I'm planning where to travel next year. I might definitely need a break after all my hard work recently, but I won't need to book something quickly or it wills get too expensive. I will go too far away, as I don't like long flights. I won't be sick of the cold weather, so I mights go somewhere hot with nice beaches. I wont spend all my time on the beach, though. I won't do some hiking as well. I'might even try surfing. It won't be fantastic! I mighty want someone to come with me. Won't you be free in February? Let me know!

Darran

↩ ↩↩   🖉 🗑

I will _____

1 _____
2 _____
3 _____
4 _____
5 _____
6 _____
7 _____
8 _____
9 _____
10 _____
11 _____

41.4 RELACIONA LAS PREGUNTAS CON SUS RESPUESTAS

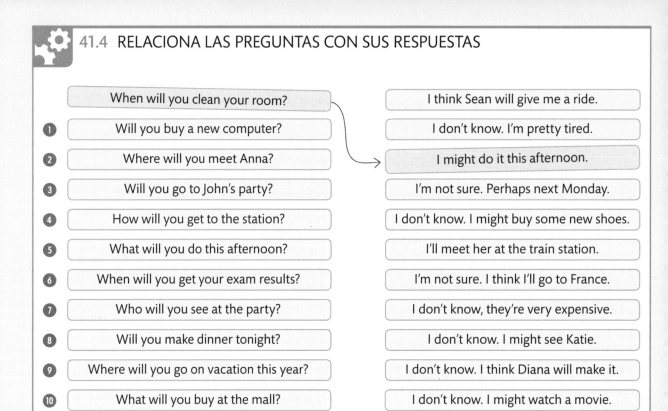

When will you clean your room?

I think Sean will give me a ride.

1. Will you buy a new computer?

I don't know. I'm pretty tired.

2. Where will you meet Anna?

I might do it this afternoon.

3. Will you go to John's party?

I'm not sure. Perhaps next Monday.

4. How will you get to the station?

I don't know. I might buy some new shoes.

5. What will you do this afternoon?

I'll meet her at the train station.

6. When will you get your exam results?

I'm not sure. I think I'll go to France.

7. Who will you see at the party?

I don't know, they're very expensive.

8. Will you make dinner tonight?

I don't know. I might see Katie.

9. Where will you go on vacation this year?

I don't know. I think Diana will make it.

10. What will you buy at the mall?

I don't know. I might watch a movie.

41.5 ESCUCHA EL AUDIO Y RESPONDE A LAS PREGUNTAS

Will John go to work today?
Yes, he will ☐
He might. ☑
No, he won't. ☐

1. Will Sally make dinner today?
Yes, she will. ☐
She might. ☐
No, she won't. ☐

2. Will Nick go to the beach?
Yes, he will. ☐
He might. ☐
No, he won't. ☐

3. Will Sara go to the movies this evening?
Yes, she will. ☐
She might. ☐
No, she won't. ☐

4. Will Jim wash his car?
Yes, he will. ☐
He might. ☐
No, he won't. ☐

5. Will Fiona go for a run this afternoon?
Yes, she will. ☐
She might. ☐
No, she won't. ☐

41.6 OBSERVA LA TABLA Y DI EN VOZ ALTA LO QUE CADA PERSONA HARÁ ("WILL"), PODRÍA HACER ("MIGHT") Y NO HARÁ ("WON'T")

	WILL	MIGHT	WON'T
Sue			
❶ Adam			
❷ Leanne			
❸ Peter			
❹ Carla			
❺ Ken			

Sue will go bungee jumping.
She might read a book.
Sue won't go to the beach.

_____ ride a bike.
_____ watch a film.
_____ cook dinner.

_____ go running.
_____ play tennis.
_____ go to bed early.

_____ drive his car.
_____ walk home.
_____ ride a motorcycle.

_____ go to the hairdresser.
_____ go to the supermarket.
_____ go swimming.

_____ have coffee.
_____ read a newspaper.
_____ eat a burger.

42 Dar consejos

Si alguien tiene un problema, una de las maneras de dar consejo es usando el verbo modal "should".

⚙ **Lenguaje** "Should"
Aa Vocabulario Consejos
🧩 **Habilidad** Dar consejos

Aa 42.1 MIRA LOS DIBUJOS Y TACHA LA PALABRA INCORRECTA DE CADA FRASE

 Peter looks very stressed. He should / ~~shouldn't~~ take a week off work.

❶ It's dark and cold outside. You should / shouldn't walk home.

❷ Tim's driving later. He should / shouldn't drink that wine.

❸ Clara is very tired. She should / shouldn't go to bed early tonight.

❹ It's very cold here. You should / shouldn't wear a sweater.

❺ Flora feels ill. She should / shouldn't go to the doctor tomorrow.

⚙ 42.2 VUELVE A ESCRIBIR LAS FRASES CORRIGIENDO LOS ERRORES

Patti should to work harder at school.
Patti should work harder at school.

❶ Carla shoulds take time off this year.

_____

❷ Casey shouldn't to buy herself a dog.

_____

❸ Kevin should saves some money for his vacation.

_____

❹ Rahul should to visit his mother more often.

_____

❺ Sherry doesn't should eat cheese late at night.

_____

42.3 ESCUCHA EL AUDIO Y MARCA EL CONSEJO CORRECTO

Carly should go away to France. ☑
Carly should go away to Finland. ☐

1 Kevin should go out with Jo. ☐
Kevin should go out with Sandra. ☐

2 Paul should wear sun lotion. ☐
Paul should wear a hat. ☐

3 Gabby should go running every day. ☐
Gabby should start a diet. ☐

4 Barry should buy a tie for his grandfather. ☐
Barry should buy socks for his grandfather. ☐

5 Murat should wear a suit for work. ☐
Murat should wear a shirt and tie. ☐

6 Phillip should read some English books. ☐
Phillip should do a language course. ☐

7 Nicky should live with a friend. ☐
Nicky should get a pet. ☐

42.4 RELACIONA LOS PROBLEMAS CON LOS CONSEJOS CORRECTOS

It's raining.

1 I have no money.

2 I don't speak English well.

3 I can't find a boyfriend.

4 I don't have any nice clothes.

5 I don't have many friends.

6 I want to lose some weight.

7 I can't sleep at night.

8 I can't wake up in the morning.

9 I want to speak perfect French.

10 I want to do well in my exams.

11 I'm feeling very stressed.

You should find a better paid job.

You should do a language course.

You should go get some coffee with my brother.

You should take an umbrella.

You should work hard at school.

You should buy an alarm clock.

You should do something relaxing before bed.

You should go jogging every evening.

You should join some clubs to meet people.

You should take a vacation.

You should live in France for a year.

You should go shopping with me next week.

43 Hacer sugerencias

Puedes utilizar el verbo modal "could" para hacer sugerencias. "Could" no es tan fuerte como "should". Sirve para dar un consejo de manera sutil.

⚙ **Lenguaje** "Could" para sugerencias
Aa Vocabulario Consejos
Habilidad Hacer sugerencias

43.1 RELACIONA LOS PROBLEMAS CON LOS CONSEJOS CORRECTOS

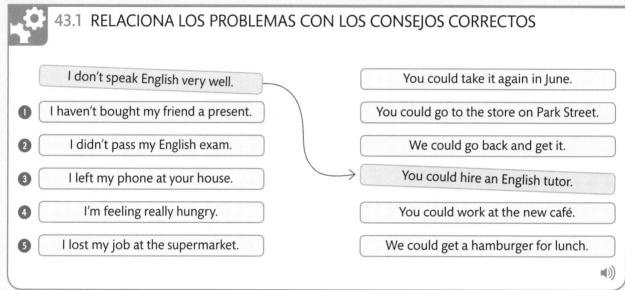

I don't speak English very well.

1 I haven't bought my friend a present.

2 I didn't pass my English exam.

3 I left my phone at your house.

4 I'm feeling really hungry.

5 I lost my job at the supermarket.

You could take it again in June.

You could go to the store on Park Street.

We could go back and get it.

You could hire an English tutor.

You could work at the new café.

We could get a hamburger for lunch.

43.2 COMPLETA LOS ESPACIOS UTILIZANDO "COULD" Y EL VERBO ENTRE PARÉNTESIS

My lecturer speaks too quickly. You _____ could ask _____ (ask) her to speak more slowly.

1 My house is too small for my family. You _____ (buy) a bigger house.

2 Jamal wants to speak better English. He _____ (practice) every day.

3 I don't know what to do when I finish school. You _____ (apply) to a college.

4 They don't have jobs right now. They _____ (look) online for a new one.

5 My sister doesn't like taking the bus. She _____ (learn) to drive herself.

43.3 ESCUCHA EL AUDIO Y MARCA LOS DOS CONSEJOS QUE SE DAN PARA CADA PROBLEMA

Jim wants to go out with Jo's sister. He could...
take her dancing ☑ **take her to a film** ☐ **take her to a café.** ☑

1 Ben wants to learn the guitar. He could...
practice at home ☐ **take lessons with a teacher** ☐ **go on a guitar vacation in Spain.** ☐

2 Jan wants to go to South America. She could...
go sailing on the Amazon ☐ **travel to Peru** ☐ **visit Buenos Aires.** ☐

3 Dave is planning to make dinner. He could...
cook some pasta ☐ **make some soup** ☐ **buy some fish.** ☐

4 Troy wants to buy his friend a present. He could...
buy her some jewelry ☐ **buy her some perfume** ☐ **get her chocolates.** ☐

43.4 COMPLETA LOS ESPACIOS UTILIZANDO LAS EXPRESIONES DEL RECUADRO, Y DI LAS FRASES EN VOZ ALTA

I can't sleep at night.

You could *read a book* .

3 I can't wake up in the morning.

You could _____ .

1 I lost my pen.

You could _____ .

4 I failed my exam.

You could _____ .

2 I don't have a girlfriend.

You could _____ .

buy a new one   ~~read a book~~

take it again

buy an alarm clock   go on a blind date

44 Vocabulario

Aa 44.1 TAREAS DOMÉSTICAS ESCRIBE LAS PALABRAS DEL RECUADRO BAJO SU IMAGEN

make the bed

1 _____

2 _____

3 _____

4 _____

7 _____

8 _____

9 _____

10 _____

11 _____

14 _____

15 _____

16 _____

17 _____

18 _____

21 _____

22 _____

23 _____

24 _____

25 _____

5 _____

6 _____

12 _____

13 _____

19 _____

20 _____

26 _____

27 _____

clean the windows   mop the floor

chop vegetables   set the table

paint a room   do the ironing

clear the table   feed the pets

wash the car   dry the dishes

vacuum the carpet   dust

mend the fence   ~~make the bed~~

hang a picture   buy groceries

walk the dog   sweep the floor

water the plants   do the gardening

scrub the floor   mow the lawn

do the laundry   fold clothes

change the sheets   cook dinner

tidy   load the dishwasher

45 La casa

Puedes utilizar el present perfect de un verbo para hablar sobre algo que ha ocurrido en el pasado y que tiene consecuencias en el presente.

Lenguaje El present perfect
Aa Vocabulario Tareas domésticas
Habilidad Hablar del pasado reciente

Aa 45.1 BUSCA OCHO PAST PARTICIPLES EN LA TABLA

```
B C W U C W E T C
C O A F L L W F L
T O S E O C R J E
I K H I S Y L F A
D E E N E W X Q N
I D D J D M E I E
E B S T A R T E D
D P A I N T E D Z
Q P F M W Y Z W S
P W M P A N V F J
S T U D I E D V I
```

study	=	studied
❶ start	=	_____
❷ close	=	_____
❸ tidy	=	_____
❹ clean	=	_____
❺ wash	=	_____
❻ paint	=	_____
❼ cook	=	_____

45.2 COMPLETA LOS ESPACIOS CON LOS VERBOS EN PRESENT PERFECT

Jenny ___has watered___ (water) the plants.

❶ Sharon _____ (mow) the lawn.

❷ You _____ (not dust) the living room.

❸ Mike _____ (paint) the walls.

❹ Mom _____ (sail) to France and Italy.

❺ I _____ (mop) the kitchen floor.

❻ He _____ (not cook) the dinner.

❼ They _____ (call) the police.

❽ We _____ (wash) the car.

❾ Jim _____ (change) the sheets.

❿ She _____ (not tidy) her room.

⓫ Karen _____ (visit) Peru.

45.3 VUELVE A ESCRIBIR LAS FRASES EN FORMA DE PREGUNTA

You have washed the car.
Have you washed the car?

1 Charlene has mopped the floor.

2 Sue has changed her sheets.

3 You have cleaned the windows.

4 Hank has tidied his bedroom.

5 Janine has cooked dinner.

6 Mrs. Underwood has visited Ireland.

7 You have started college.

8 Sid has walked to school.

9 She has called her grandmother.

10 You have watched this film.

11 Adam has painted his bedroom.

◀))

45.4 VUELVE A ESCRIBIR LAS FRASES CORRIGIENDO LOS ERRORES

Greg **haven't** washed his clothes.
Greg hasn't washed his clothes.

1 Katy **haven't** cleaned the bathroom.

2 We **hasn't** left school.

3 I **hasn't** tidied the kitchen.

4 My mom **haven't** read the letter.

5 We **hasn't** painted the backyard fence.

6 James **haven't** tidied his bedroom.

7 You **hasn't** cooked the dinner.

8 Terry **haven't** visited the US.

9 Anne **haven't** been to London.

◀))

45.5 COMPLETA LOS ESPACIOS PONIENDO LOS VERBOS EN PRESENT PERFECT

They ___have left___ (leave) the house.

1 Peter _____ (win) the race.

2 We _____ (eat) all the pastries.

3 Michelle _____ (start) a new job.

4 We _____ (finish) our chores.

5 Dave _____ (keep) a seat for you.

6 I _____ (spend) all my money.

7 Chan _____ (break) the window.

8 They _____ (give) Grandpa new slippers.

9 Jacob _____ (hear) the bad news.

10 Mr. Evans _____ (leave) the building.

11 Mike _____ (put) the cup away.

12 He _____ (tell) me about life in the 1960s.

13 Antoine _____ (teach) me French.

14 Craig _____ (write) a novel.

15 Doug _____ (see) that movie twice.

16 We _____ (be) in France for three weeks.

17 Abe _____ (fly) to Paris for the weekend.

18 You _____ (forgot) my birthday again!

19 I _____ (find) a new job.

20 Zac _____ (do) his homework.

21 Hugh _____ (drive) to work today.

22 She _____ (take) her son to school.

23 Owen _____ (buy) a new shirt.

◀))

45.6 ESCUCHA EL AUDIO Y RESPONDE A LAS PREGUNTAS

Has Sally been to the new café?
Yes, she has. ☑ **No, she hasn't.** ☐

1 Has Peter finished the book?
Yes, he has. ☐ **No, he hasn't.** ☐

2 Have Chloe and Jake finished the report?
Yes, they have. ☐ **No, they haven't.** ☐

3 Has Douglas ever visited Peru?
Yes, he has. ☐ **No, he hasn't.** ☐

4 Has Flo had her lunch?
Yes, she has. ☐ **No, she hasn't.** ☐

5 Has Jenny seen the new spy movie?
Yes, she has. ☐ **No, she hasn't.** ☐

6 Has Peter been to the gym this week?
Yes, he has. ☐ **No, he hasn't.** ☐

7 Has Roger bought a present?
Yes, he has. ☐ **No, he hasn't.** ☐

45.7 COMPLETA LOS ESPACIOS PONIENDO LOS VERBOS DEL RECUADRO EN PRESENT PERFECT

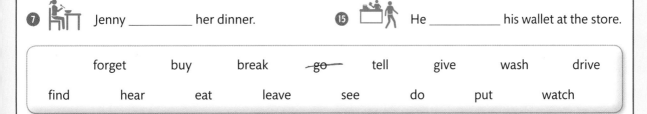

Pete _has gone_ to school.

❶ They _____ me the news.

❷ You _____ my name again!

❸ Sim _____ the news.

❹ Derek _____ a new tie.

❺ John _____ his homework.

❻ We _____ that movie twice.

❼ Jenny _____ her dinner.

❽ Amy _____ me a nice present.

❾ I _____ my shirt in the closet.

❿ He _____ his watch under the bed.

⓫ The children _____ the window.

⓬ They _____ the soccer game.

⓭ Jo _____ the car.

⓮ Tom _____ the dishes.

⓯ He _____ his wallet at the store.

forget	buy	break	~~go~~	tell	give	wash	drive
find	hear	eat	leave	see	do	put	watch

45.8 UTILIZA EL DIAGRAMA PARA CREAR 12 FRASES CORRECTAS Y DILAS EN VOZ ALTA

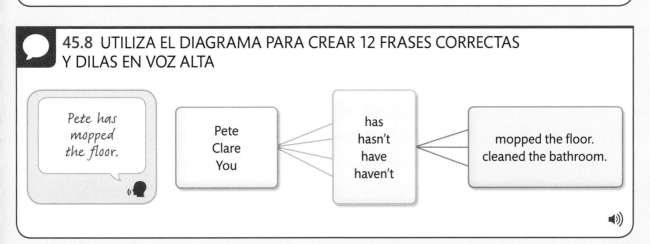

Pete has mopped the floor.

| Pete / Clare / You | has / hasn't / have / haven't | mopped the floor. / cleaned the bathroom. |

46 Acontecimientos de tu vida

Tanto el present perfect como el past simple pueden utilizarse para hablar de cosas que han ocurrido en el pasado, pero los usamos de manera diferente.

⚙ **Lenguaje** El present perfect
Aa Vocabulario Deportes de aventura
🏃 **Habilidad** Hablar de acontecimientos pasados

46.1 TACHA LAS PALABRAS INCORRECTAS DE CADA FRASE

Logan goes surfing every year. He ~~went~~ / has been surfing in Hawaii six times.

1 **Did you go** / Have you been to work yesterday? There was an important meeting at 11 am.

2 Mom **made** / has made a birthday cake for Samantha last weekend. It was delicious.

3 Owen went to Spain last month. He **sent** / has sent us a postcard of Madrid.

4 I love the film *Trip to Heaven*. I **saw** / have seen it five times.

5 Deena **visited** / has visited both the Grand Canyon and Monument Valley in Arizona.

🔊

46.2 RESPONDE AL AUDIO EN VOZ ALTA UTILIZANDO LOS TIEMPOS VERBALES CORRECTOS

Have you ever been snorkeling?

Yes, *I've been snorkeling* many times.

🗣

1 Have you ever been surfing?

Yes, _____ many times.

🗣

2 Have you ever been to China?

Yes, _____ there in 2014.

🗣

3 Have any of your family been to the US?

Yes, my dad _____ twice.

🗣

4 Have you ever seen *Casablanca*?

No, _____ it.

🗣

5 Has your brother ever done a bungee jump?

Yes, _____ last year.

🗣

🔊

46.3 COMPLETA LOS ESPACIOS PONIENDO LOS VERBOS EN SU TIEMPO CORRECTO

46.3 COMPLETA LOS ESPACIOS PONIENDO LOS VERBOS EN SU TIEMPO CORRECTO

> Sam went paragliding last summer and in 2013. He ___*has been*___ (be) paragliding twice.

1 Fran has been to France many times. She _____ (visit) France last summer.

2 David went rock-climbing in 2013 and 2014. He _____ (be) rock-climbing twice.

3 Cam went bungee-jumping last summer. She _____ (be) bungee-jumping once.

4 Jamie goes surfing most weekends. He _____ (go) surfing yesterday.

5 Rachel climbed Mount Fuji in 2013 and 2014. She _____ (climb) it twice.

6 Jim went diving in Egypt last summer and spring. He _____ (be) diving there twice.

7 I went wing-walking in New Zealand last year. It _____ (be) amazing!

8 My brother went paragliding last summer. He _____ (be) paragliding once.

9 Archie goes snowboarding every winter. He _____ (be) snowboarding eight times.

10 My cousin goes caving most weekends. I _____ (never be) caving.

11 Ray goes windsurfing most weekends. He _____ (go) windsurfing today.

12 My brother loves racing. He _____ (race) in many competitions.

13 I have skied in Austria three times. I _____ (go) skiing there last winter.

14 Tom loves kitesurfing. He _____ (be) kitesurfing in many different countries.

🔊

46.4 LEE LA POSTAL Y ESCRIBE LOS VERBOS EN LA LISTA CORRECTA

Hi Anna,

We're in New York! We got here four days ago and have seen lots of things. On Tuesday we visited the Statue of Liberty and on Wednesday we went shopping. I have been to Macy's department store, finally! We have had some great food. Last night we ate at a Vietnamese restaurant. It was great. Today we have visited MOMA, the modern art museum. It has been a wonderful trip.

Love,

Harry

PRESENT PERFECT

have seen

① _____

② _____

③ _____

④ _____

PAST SIMPLE

got

⑤ _____

⑥ _____

⑦ _____

⑧ _____

46.5 COMPLETA LOS ESPACIOS CON "BEEN" O "GONE"

There's lots of food in the fridge because Ayida's _____ been _____ to the supermarket.

① I love Florence. I've _____ there three times.

② Tina has _____ to Spain. She'll be back in two weeks.

③ Have you ever _____ skiing in Norway?

④ I've _____ to the new museum in town. It's very crowded.

⑤ John and Kate have _____ to the theater. They're meeting you there.

⑥ I have _____ to Hero's to meet some friends. See you there later.

🔊

46.6 ESCUCHA EL AUDIO Y RESPONDE A LAS PREGUNTAS

Martin and Nigel had a great time in Australia.
True ☑ **False** ☐ **Not given** ☐

1 Mary has been to Florida.
True ☐ **False** ☐ **Not given** ☐

2 Tony has never visited Paris.
True ☐ **False** ☐ **Not given** ☐

3 Sarah went to Japan in 2014.
True ☐ **False** ☐ **Not given** ☐

4 Ben has been windsurfing many times.
True ☐ **False** ☐ **Not given** ☐

5 Anne has never been to London.
True ☐ **False** ☐ **Not given** ☐

6 Steve went paragliding in Portugal.
True ☐ **False** ☐ **Not given** ☐

7 Janet has been to Machu Picchu.
True ☐ **False** ☐ **Not given** ☐

46.7 COMPLETA LOS ESPACIOS PONIENDO LOS VERBOS EN SU TIEMPO CORRECTO

I _____*got*_____ (get) my first job five years ago.

1 Larry and Michel _____ (go) to the US twice in 2014.

2 Hannah _____ (dive) in Australia many times.

3 Jim and Rose _____ (make) a cake last weekend.

4 Debbie _____ (never be) to India. She would like to go there one day.

5 Jim _____ (be) to Japan twice. He loved it.

6 I _____ (not try) windsurfing, but I'd like to!

7 Jack _____ (go) to a movie, I'm not sure when he'll be back.

145

Uno de los usos del present perfect es hablar de hechos en un periodo de tiempo que aún no ha finalizado. Utiliza el past simple para periodos de tiempo que ya han finalizado.

⚙ **Lenguaje** "Yet" y "already"
Aa Vocabulario Rutinas y tareas
Habilidad Hablar del pasado reciente

 47.1 COMPLETA LOS ESPACIOS PONIENDO EL VERBO EN PRESENT PERFECT O PAST SIMPLE

I _____*saw*_____ (see) a new movie on Thursday.

❶ I _____ (be) to five countries on vacation this year.

❷ Sandra _____ (pass) all her medical exams so far this year. I'm so proud.

❸ I _____ (visit) Warsaw in 2007 with my family.

❹ I'm feeling sleepy. I _____ (not have) any coffee yet this morning.

❺ My boyfriend _____ (phone) me last night.

❻ Paula's feeling sad. Her dog _____ (die) last week.

❼ I'm going to Berlin tomorrow. I _____ (be) there three times before.

❽ I don't have any money. I _____ (lose) my wallet yesterday.

❾ This is such a good festival. I _____ (make) lots of new friends.

❿ My sister is really happy. She _____ (pass) her driving test yesterday.

⓫ I _____ (play) tennis six times this week. And I'm playing again tomorrow.

🔊

47.2 LEE EL ARTÍCULO Y RESPONDE A LAS PREGUNTAS CON FRASES COMPLETAS

> Where does Rick live?
>
> _He lives in Wellington, New Zealand._

1 How many gold medals has Rick won?

_____

2 What happened at the World Championships?

_____

3 When is the next world athletics event?

_____

4 When did Rick first become famous?

_____

5 What has Rick done with his free time?

_____

FAMOUS PEOPLE

The long wait

Rick Clay talks about his plans to get back on track

Rick Clay is one of the world's top athletes. He lives in Wellington, New Zealand. Rick has won five gold medals in the last four years. This year has been very difficult for Rick, however. After he injured himself in the World Championships in Athens in June, Rick hasn't run in any more races.

"It's been a very frustrating year. I'm getting better, but it takes time."

The next world athletics event is in Sydney in December. "I really want to go. But I'm not sure if my knee will be ready."

Rick first became famous five years ago when he broke the 400m world record. Rick has tried to be positive about his health problems. "I've done lots of gardening and I've spent more time with my family. So that's good."

 47.3 VUELVE A ESCRIBIR LAS FRASES CORRIGIENDO LOS ERRORES

> I have be to Moscow this year.
>
> _I have been to Moscow this year._

1 We has never eaten Chinese food.

_____

2 Sharon have seen that movie before.

_____

3 I have play cricket three times in my life.

_____

4 Natasha has visit Rio de Janeiro three times.

_____

5 Yuri hasn't phone his grandmother.

_____

6 Eddy have bought a new car for his son.

_____

7 Karen is forgotten her ticket for the concert.

_____

Aa 47.4 RELACIONA LAS FRASES QUE VAN JUNTAS

Have you read this book?

No, the game hasn't started yet.

1. Can you tell Samantha about the party?

I've already told her.

2. Has Rico taken his exam?

He's already arrived.

3. Am I too late for the game?

Yes, I've already read it.

4. What time is Dewain arriving?

It's already landed.

5. I'll order the taxi now.

Sorry, I haven't started it yet.

6. Has the plane from Lisbon landed?

I've already ordered it!

7. Has Claire finished her exercises?

No, he hasn't taken it yet.

8. Have you done your project?

Yes, they've already left.

9. Have Bob and Jane gone back home?

No, she hasn't done them yet.

47.5 ESCUCHA EL AUDIO Y RESPONDE A LAS PREGUNTAS

Sue y Jim se preparan para ir a una fiesta y comprueban que lo tienen todo.

Jim hasn't made the sandwiches yet.
True ☑ **False** ☐

1. Sue has already bought some bread.
True ☐ **False** ☐

2. Sue hasn't bought any ham or cheese yet.
True ☐ **False** ☐

3. Jim has already bought some avocados.
True ☐ **False** ☐

4. Sue has already bought some wine.
True ☐ **False** ☐

5. Jim hasn't bought any juice or soda yet.
True ☐ **False** ☐

6. Jim has borrowed Danny's wireless speaker.
True ☐ **False** ☐

7. Jim hasn't bought the cake yet.
True ☐ **False** ☐

47.6 COMPLETA LOS ESPACIOS CON "ALREADY" O "YET"

The play has _____already_____ started.

1 I've _____ read that book.

2 I haven't seen the new movie _____ .

3 Chrissie has _____ left for work.

4 The soccer game hasn't started _____ .

5 I haven't passed my test _____ .

6 I've _____ visited that castle twice.

7 Has the party started _____ ?

8 I've _____ ordered the taxi.

9 Malik has _____ emailed Dan.

10 Has Terry cleaned his room _____ ?

11 Tony's _____ made the sandwiches.

12 I've _____ ordered pizza for everyone.

13 Julia hasn't cooked the dinner _____ .

14 She hasn't been to London _____ .

15 Ali has _____ bought some milk.

16 Has Tim phoned his grandmother _____ ?

17 Sanjay hasn't sold his car _____ .

🔊

47.7 OBSERVA LA LISTA DE TAREAS Y ESCRIBE RESPUESTAS A LAS PREGUNTAS UTILIZANDO "ALREADY" O "YET"

Has Sarah cleaned her room yet?

She's already cleaned her room.

1 Has she walked the dog yet?

_____

2 Has she sent the emails yet?

_____

3 Has Sarah bought the fruit and vegetables yet?

_____

4 Has she bought a present for Claire yet?

_____

5 Has she phoned the bank yet?

_____

TO DO...

~~Clean my room~~
Walk the dog
Send some emails
~~Buy some fruit and vegetables~~
~~Buy a present for Claire~~
Phone the bank

149

48 Comer fuera

"Eating out" significa comer fuera de casa, habitualmente en un restaurante. Para hacerlo, debes conocer las frases necesarias para hacer una reserva o pedir comida.

⚙ **Lenguaje** Frases de restaurante
Aa Vocabulario Preparación de la comida
🧩 **Habilidad** Pedir comida en un restaurante

Aa 48.1 CONECTA LOS DIBUJOS CON LOS PEDIDOS CORRECTOS

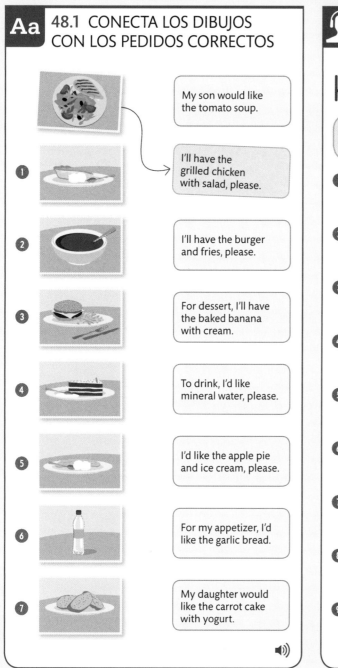

My son would like the tomato soup.

I'll have the grilled chicken with salad, please.

❶

I'll have the burger and fries, please.

❷

For dessert, I'll have the baked banana with cream.

❸

To drink, I'd like mineral water, please.

❹

I'd like the apple pie and ice cream, please.

❺

For my appetizer, I'd like the garlic bread.

❻

My daughter would like the carrot cake with yogurt.

❼

🔊

48.2 ESCUCHA EL AUDIO Y RESPONDE A LAS PREGUNTAS

Dos personas piden su comida en un restaurante.

The couple have booked a table.
True ☑ False ☐

❶ The couple ask for a table next to the window.
True ☐ False ☐

❷ The couple don't want to see the wine list.
True ☐ False ☐

❸ They order when the waiter comes back.
True ☐ False ☐

❹ The man orders bean soup.
True ☐ False ☐

❺ The woman orders green salad.
True ☐ False ☐

❻ The man orders a special.
True ☐ False ☐

❼ The woman would like fish.
True ☐ False ☐

❽ The couple ask for a bottle of red wine.
True ☐ False ☐

❾ The couple both want the same dessert.
True ☐ False ☐

48.3 LEE LA CARTA Y RESPONDE A LAS PREGUNTAS

The restaurant has a separate menu for

Vegetarians ☐
Children ☑
Meat eaters ☐

❶ Which appetizer can be shared by two people?

The soup ☐
The salad ☐
The antipasti ☐

❷ What do you get with the onion tart?

Garlic bread ☐
New potatoes ☐
Tomato and pepper soup ☐

❸ Which of the chef's specials is for vegetarians?

The roast chicken ☐
The fish of the day ☐
The spaghetti ☐

❹ How much is the chocolate pudding?

$4.50 ☐
$4.95 ☐
$5.95 ☐

ADAM'S KITCHEN

For children's meals, see separate menu.

APPETIZERS

Roast tomato and pepper soup (V)	$3.95
Mediterranean salad with grilled baby vegetables (V)	$4.95
Antipasti: Cold meats, cheese, and olives (2 people)	$9.95

ENTRÉES

All main courses (not specials) come with new potatoes.

Onion and bean tart with a green salad (V)	$7.95
Beef and ale pie with onion gravy	$8.95
Spicy pasta with tomato and cheese (V)	$6.95

CHEF'S SPECIALS

Whole roast chicken with roast potatoes	$8.95
Grilled fish of the day with fries and peas	$9.95
Spaghetti with a cream and vegetable sauce (V)	$7.95

DESSERTS

Lemon cheesecake	$4.50
Chocolate pudding (V)	$4.95
Strawberry cake and vanilla ice cream	$4.50

(V) = suitable for vegetarians

48.4 UTILIZA EL DIAGRAMA PARA CREAR NUEVE FRASES CORRECTAS Y DILAS EN VOZ ALTA

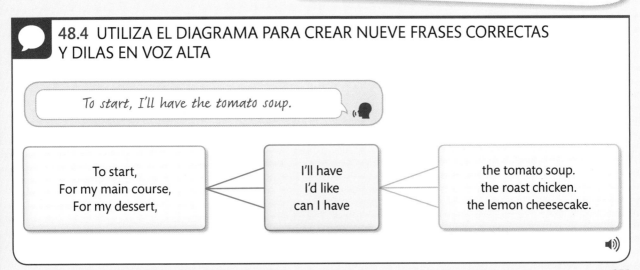

Logros y ambiciones

En inglés se utilizan diferentes expresiones para hablar sobre deseos futuros, planes de futuro definidos y logros pasados. Puedes emplearlas al hablar de tu vida.

🔧 **Lenguaje** Deseos y planes
Aa Vocabulario Viajes y deportes de aventura
🏃 **Habilidad** Hablar de tus logros

Aa 49.1 RELACIONA LAS PREGUNTAS CON LAS RESPUESTAS CORRECTAS

Have you ever been to Kyoto?

1 Have you ever played soccer?

2 Have you ever worked abroad?

3 Have you ever won the lottery?

4 Have you ever seen a ghost?

5 Have you ever been to Italy?

6 Have you ever played the piano?

7 Have you ever fallen off your bike?

8 Have you ever been on TV?

9 Have you ever seen a lion?

10 Have you ever visited New York?

11 Have you ever had a pet?

12 Have you ever been sky diving?

13 Have you ever seen *Shrek*?

14 Have you ever been to Paris?

15 Have you ever tried Indian food?

Yes, but I prefer rugby.

Yes, I was an English teacher in China.

Yes, I was on a news program.

No, but we're going to Japan next year.

No, I'm scared of heights.

Yes, it's a really funny movie.

Yes, I saw the Eiffel Tower.

Yes, I love curry.

Yes, when I was at the zoo.

Yes, I had a cat when I was young.

Yes, I was in Rome last year.

Yes, I once won $10.

Yes. I was really scared!

No, but I'd like to see the Statue of Liberty.

Yes, I played the piano at school.

Yes, I broke my arm.

49.2 ESCUCHA EL AUDIO Y MARCA LO QUE NIGEL HA HECHO YA O NO

Has done ✓ Hasn't done ☐

1 Has done ☐ Hasn't done ☐

2 Has done ☐ Hasn't done ☐

3 Has done ☐ Hasn't done ☐

4 Has done ☐ Hasn't done ☐

5 Has done ☐ Hasn't done ☐

Aa 49.3 COMPLETA LOS ESPACIOS CON LAS PALABRAS DEL RECUADRO

Melinda will _____ fly _____ to Moscow tomorrow.

1 My _____ leaves at 5am from London.

2 I want to _____ for treasure in the Pacific Ocean.

3 He learned to _____ in California.

4 My _____ got lost when I changed flights.

5 I checked into the _____ at 10pm.

surf

luggage

fly

flight

dive

hotel

153

49.4 COMPLETA LOS ESPACIOS PARA DECIR LO QUE CADA PERSONA NO HA HECHO Y LO QUE QUIERE HACER

Gloria __has never been__ (never / be) to Venice, but she __really wants__ (really / want) to go there.

1 We _____ (never / see) a Shakespeare play, but we _____ (really / want) to see one.

2 Steve _____ (never / play) a musical instrument, but he _____ (really / want) to learn one.

3 I _____ (never / write) a novel, but I _____ (really / want) to do so one day.

4 Esteban _____ (never / eat) Chinese food, but he _____ (really / want) to try some.

5 Ethan _____ (never / see) a wolf, but he _____ (really / want) to photograph one.

6 Stef _____ (never / play) golf, but she _____ (really / want) to try it one day.

7 Tommy _____ (never / be) to America, but he _____ (really / want) to go there.

8 They _____ (never / stay) in a hotel, but they _____ (really / want) to.

9 Doug _____ (never / ride) a horse, but he _____ (really / want) to try it.

10 Marge _____ (never / win) the lottery, but she _____ (really / want) to someday.

11 Kimberley _____ (never / fly) in an airplane, but she _____ (really / want) to do it.

12 Landon _____ (never / climb) a mountain, but he _____ (really / want) to visit the Rockies.

13 Our children _____ (never / be) to a movie theater, but they _____ (really / want) to go.

14 We _____ (never / travel) around South America, but we _____ (really / want) to.

15 Olivia _____ (never / eat) olives, but she _____ (really / want) to try them.

16 I _____ (never / see) an action movie, but I _____ (really / want) to see one.

17 Emily _____ (never / swim) in the ocean, but she _____ (really / want) to try it.

18 Melvin _____ (never / do) a parachute jump, but he _____ (really / want) to do one.

19 Pete _____ (never / see) a tiger, but he _____ (really / want) to travel to India.

20 Patti _____ (never / be) to the theater, but she _____ (really / want) to go.

21 Mary _____ (never / leave) her country, but she _____ (really / want) to travel abroad.

◀))

Aa 49.5 RELACIONA LOS DIBUJOS CON LAS FRASES CORRECTAS

I've never swum in the ocean, but my wife and I are going to Tahiti for our anniversary.

I've never been skiing, but my husband's taking me to Switzerland for my birthday in February.

I've never tried Chinese food, but my colleagues are taking me to a restaurant in Chinatown next week.

My boyfriend's never been to Paris, but I'm taking him there for his birthday.

My daughter's never seen a tiger, but we're taking her to the zoo on the weekend.

49.6 UTILIZA EL DIAGRAMA PARA CREAR OCHO FRASES CORRECTAS Y DILAS EN VOZ ALTA

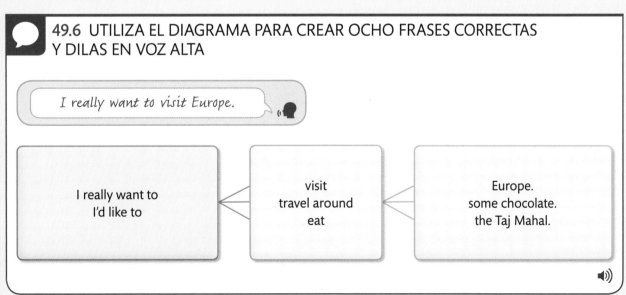

I really want to visit Europe.

| I really want to I'd like to | visit travel around eat | Europe. some chocolate. the Taj Mahal. |

Respuestas

01

1.1 🔊
1. They **are** the Walker family.
2. You **are** a police officer.
3. Eve **is** from Canada.
4. I **am** a teacher.
5. We **are** Australian.
6. He **is** an artist.

1.2 🔊
1. They **are** doctors.
2. I **am** from Canada.
3. Elizabeth **is** British.
4. You **are** a mechanic.
5. Luke **is** an engineer.
6. She **is** 35 years old.

1.3 🔊
1. We are French.
2. We are chefs.
3. I am French.
4. She is French.
5. I am Anita.
6. She is Anita.
7. I am an actor.
8. She is an actor.

1.4 🔊 Nota: Todas las respuestas pueden también escribirse en su forma contraída.
1. John and Ellie **are not** best friends.
2. Mr. Robbins **is not** a teacher.
3. It **is not** 2 o'clock.
4. You **are not** my sister.
5. Annabelle **is not** at school.
6. Ann and Ravi **are not** students.
7. Ken **is not** a mechanic.
8. We **are not** doctors.
9. He **is not** 45 years old.
10. They **are not** my teachers.
11. She **is not** from Ireland.
12. It **is not** Martha's book.

1.5 🔊
1. This **is not** the bank.
2. You **are not** a gardener.
3. Selma **is not** a teacher.

4. We **are not** from Spain.
5. I **am not** at home.
6. They **are not** 20 years old.

1.6 🔊
1. **Are** they your dogs?
2. **Is** Jo your cousin?
3. **Is** it 10 o'clock?
4. **Am** I in your class?
5. **Are** you Canadian?
6. **Are** those your keys?
7. **Is** Martin at work today?
8. **Is** Elena 28 years old?
9. **Are** they nurses?

02

2.1 🔊
1. They **cook** pizza for dinner.
2. Your friend **has** a microwave.
3. She **works** at the gym.
4. I **watch** TV every day.
5. We **leave** work at 5pm.
6. Mark **has** a skateboard.
7. They **start** school at 9am.
8. You **hate** soccer.
9. Tara **eats** breakfast at 7:15am.
10. I **go** to the park after work.
11. We **wake up** at 7am.
12. He **cooks** dinner at 8pm.
13. My son **walks** to school.

2.2 🔊
1. Laura **watches** TV all day.
2. You **wake up** at 7am.
3. I **leave** work at 6pm.
4. My cousins **go** to the gym.
5. She **has** a laptop.
6. James **works** in a bank.
7. They **eat** lunch at 1:30pm.

2.3 🔊
1. They **eat** pizza for lunch.
2. Mia **gets up** late on Saturdays.
3. You **go** to work early.
4. We **cook** dinner at 7:30pm.
5. Paul **finishes** work at 6pm.
6. Lily **watches** TV every day.
7. They **start** work at 10am.
8. Robert **has** a car.
9. I **wake up** at 6:45am.
10. Jay **studies** science every day.

11. Karen **likes** tennis.
12. He **works** in a school.
13. Jess **goes** to bed at 10pm.

2.4
A. 4
B. 1
C. 5
D. 2
E. 6
F. 3

2.5
1. False 2. True 3. Not given 4. True
5. True 6. False

2.6 🔊
1. We eat lunch **at 1:30 every day.**
2. Katia wakes up at **6:30 every morning.**
3. My parents have **two cats and a dog.**
4. Dave watches **TV in the evening.**
5. I walk to work **every day.**
6. You work in **an office in town.**

2.7
1. I do not work in a school.
   I don't work in a school.
2. Sam eats lunch at 1pm.
   Sam doesn't eat lunch at 1pm.
3. We leave home at 7:45am.
   We do not leave home at 7:45am.
4. They do not like pizza.
   They don't like pizza.
5. Sia watches TV every day.
   Sia doesn't watch TV every day.
6. My friend has a dog.
   My friend does not have a dog.
7. You do not get up early.
   You don't get up early.
8. I have a new coat.
   I don't have a new coat.
9. He finishes work at 5:30pm.
   He does not finish work at 5:30pm.

2.8 🔊
1. Lucy doesn't walk to work.
2. Lucy doesn't get up early.
3. Lucy doesn't eat breakfast.
4. I don't walk to work.
5. I don't get up early.
6. I don't eat breakfast.
7. They don't walk to work.
8. They don't get up early.
9. They don't eat breakfast.

10. Do you like cats?

11. Do you like soccer?

12. Do you work in an office?

13. Does John like cats?

14. Does John like soccer?

15. Does John work in an office?

03

3.1 🔊

1. Glen **is** cleaning his car.
2. April **is** watching a film.
3. Peter and Frank **are** wearing suits.
4. James **is** painting the kitchen.
5. We **are** traveling around China.
6. You **are** listening to an interesting song.
7. Doug **is** reading a newspaper.

3.2

Ⓐ 3

Ⓑ 5

Ⓒ 1

Ⓓ 6

Ⓔ 2

Ⓕ 4

3.3 🔊

1. Anne **is waiting** for her brother.
2. Pedro **is cooking** pizza for dinner.
3. Mike **is mowing** the lawn.
4. Cynthia **is lying** on the sofa.
5. Jane **is going** to the theater.
6. I **am working** at the moment.
7. Colin **is listening** to some music.
8. Our children **are playing** in a band.
9. We **are drinking** lemonade.
10. Stefan **is coming** to our party.
11. They **are eating** pasta for dinner.
12. Roberta **is wearing** a sweater.
13. You **are playing** tennis with John.

3.4 🔊

1. Paula doesn't often watch TV, **but tonight she's watching a good movie.**
2. Sven usually cooks at home, **but today he's eating at a restaurant.**
3. I often go to bed at 11pm, **but this evening I'm going to bed early.**
4. Janet is working at home today, **but she usually works in an office.**
5. Ravi usually wears casual clothes, **but today he's wearing a business suit.**

6. Tim usually has cereal for breakfast, **but this morning he's having eggs.**
7. We usually go on vacation to Greece, **but this year we're visiting Italy.**
8. I almost always drive to work, **but today I'm walking as my car won't start.**
9. Nelson is drinking wine today, **but he normally drinks beer.**
10. You usually wear pants, **but today you're wearing a skirt.**

3.5 🔊

1. Vlad **isn't** playing soccer.
2. We **aren't** working today.
3. Manek **isn't** wearing a tie.
4. We **aren't** coming to the party.
5. Clarice **isn't** having dinner today.
6. Jonathan **isn't** walking the dog.
7. Mark and Trevor **aren't** going to the theater.
8. Pedro **isn't** wearing a suit.
9. Sally and Clive **aren't** going on vacation.
10. Sebastian **isn't** watching the movie.
11. You **aren't** working hard enough.

3.6 🔊

1. Angelica isn't watching TV.
2. I'm working at home.
3. We aren't playing soccer.
4. Ginny is eating a burger.
5. Sharon isn't listening to music.
6. They are drinking soda.
7. We aren't going shopping.
8. Anita is visiting Athens.
9. Pete isn't playing tennis.
10. You are speaking Dutch.
11. Paul isn't wearing a hat.
12. I am walking home.
13. Steven isn't going swimming.

3.7 🔊

1. Kate isn't going on vacation this year.
2. Tracy is taking the dog for a walk.
3. Irena isn't coming to the party.
4. We are walking to school today.
5. Trevor is cooking his dinner.
6. Mr. Smith is traveling to Singapore.
7. They aren't playing soccer today.
8. I am buying a new pair of shoes.
9. You aren't wearing a coat today.

3.8 🔊

1. Jenny is wearing pants.
2. Gemma isn't driving to work.
3. We are singing.
4. Brendan is eating a burger.
5. Sal is wearing a long coat.
6. Mo is watching a movie.
7. Emily is wearing glasses.
8. Jo is listening to music.
9. Kate is wearing a skirt.

04

4.1 🔊

1. What is he reading? **A book.**
2. Where are you going? **To the library.**
3. Who is talking? **Sue and Johnny.**
4. Why is she shouting? **She's angry.**
5. What is he wearing? **A suit and tie.**
6. What are the children doing? **Playing computer games.**

4.2 🔊

1. Lenny is **wearing** a tie today.
2. Sarah is **cooking** dinner.
3. Frank is **running** in the park.
4. Jane is **walking** the dog.
5. Simon is **listening** to music.
6. Pat is **driving** to work.
7. Gavin is **eating** breakfast.

4.3

1. Diane
2. Tommy
3. Jo
4. Alex
5. Jean
6. George
7. Isabel
8. Ray
9. Louise
10. Jon

4.4 🔊

1. I **am doing** my English homework.
2. He **is making** breakfast.
3. She **is reading** a magazine.
4. They **are running** by the river.
5. I **am writing** an email.
6. We **are listening** to music.
7. She **is driving** to London.
8. He **is taking** a bath.

9 They **are doing** the shopping.
10 I **am eating** a pizza.
11 You **are riding** a motorcycle.
12 We **are going** to bed.

4.5 🔊
1 What is Kay watching?
2 What is Dan eating?
3 What are Tim and Jay playing?
4 What is Sara wearing?
5 What are you carrying?
6 What is Charlie listening to?
7 What is Sharon drinking?
8 What is Sam making?
9 What are you writing?

4.6 🔊
1 Where is Kim going?
2 Who are you phoning?
3 Why are you crying?
4 When are you meeting John?
5 What are you cooking?
6 Where is your band playing?
7 Why are you shouting?
8 What are you drinking?
9 How are you getting to the concert?

4.7
1 Claude
2 Robert
3 Peter's mom
4 Pedro
5 Dan

4.8 🔊
1 **They are drinking** some coffee.
2 **Meg is eating** a pizza.
3 **Louise is riding** a horse.
4 **Paul is using** his computer.
5 **Philippa is baking** a cake.

05

5.1
VERBOS DE ACCIÓN
eat, sing, learn, play, go, listen
VERBOS DE ESTADO
have, love, want, remember, know, hate

5.2 🔊
1 I remember it is your birthday today.
2 Dan wants a drink.

3 You have two sisters.
4 He owns this house.
5 My brother loves Anne.
6 We own a horse.
7 My dad hates pizza.

5.3 🔊
1 Greg **is playing** tennis now.
2 Mo **is watching** TV right now.
3 We **have** a new dog.
4 You **don't like** snakes.
5 Dom **is going** to school now.

5.4
1 Jane **works** at the school near her apartment.
2 Jane really **likes** teaching.
3 Jane **goes** to restaurants on the weekend.
4 Jane **has** three children.
5 Ben **is playing** soccer with his friends.
6 Silvia **is watching** a film at the movie theater.
7 Mike **is listening** to music in his room.

5.5 🔊
1 Samantha has three children.
2 They're running to school.
3 She hates snakes.
4 She's listening to music.

06

6.1 🔊
1 stressed
2 lonely
3 unhappy
4 bored
5 curious
6 distracted
7 angry
8 worried
9 tired
10 jealous
11 excited
12 calm
13 relaxed
14 confident
15 disappointed
16 scared
17 grateful
18 amused
19 irritated

20 confused
21 proud
22 surprised
23 anxious

07

7.1
excited, nervous, bored, pleased, bad, calm, happy, sad, angry, tired

---

7.2 🔊
1 Alexander is feeling **excited**.
2 Danny is feeling **tired**.
3 Peter is feeling **proud**.
4 Samantha is feeling **sad**.
5 I'm feeling **happy**.
6 Christopher is feeling **curious**.
7 Waldo is feeling **bored**.

7.3 🔊
1 Claire is feeling happy because it's her birthday.
2 Marge is feeling annoyed because Jack is being naughty.
3 Shaun is feeling excited because he's watching soccer.
4 Chris is feeling tired because it's very late.
5 Angelo is feeling bored because his book isn't interesting.
6 Sandy is feeling jealous because her sister has a new toy.
7 Rachel is feeling nervous because she has an exam.
8 Carl is feeling sad because he misses his dog.
9 Anne is feeling angry because her boyfriend is late.
10 Jimmy is feeling pleased because he has a new car.
11 Ron is feeling relaxed because he is on vacation.

7.4 🔊
1. I am feeling nervous.
2. I am feeling happy.
3. I am feeling sad.
4. Jim is feeling nervous.
5. Jim is feeling happy.
6. Jim is feeling sad.
7. We are feeling nervous.
8. We are feeling happy.
9. We are feeling sad.

10. They are feeling nervous.
11. They are feeling happy.
12. They are feeling sad.

7.5
1 Charles is feeling scared.
2 Colin is feeling sad.
3 Jim is feeling nervous.
4 Greg is feeling annoyed.
5 Tanya is feeling tired.
6 Bill and Susan are feeling excited.
7 Giles is feeling happy.
8 Arnold is feeling relaxed.
9 Katy is feeling bored.

7.6 ◀))
1 Evie is really angry. **The bus still hasn't arrived.**
2 Peter is feeling very tired today. **So he's staying in bed.**
3 Jenny is so nervous. **She has an exam tomorrow.**
4 Danny is feeling really dissapointed. **He didn't win the competition.**
5 Angelo is so bored. **He wants something to do.**

7.7 ◀))
1 It's my birthday tomorrow. I really can't wait! I'm so **excited**.
2 I don't like this house. It's so dark. Is that a spider? I'm feeling very **scared**.
3 I don't know what to do. There's nothing on TV. I'm really **bored**.
4 This book is really depressing. So many bad things happen. I'm feeling really **sad**.
5 My girlfriend's forgotten my birthday. And she forgot last year. I'm so **angry**.

08

8.1 ◀))
1 boat
2 train station
3 port
4 taxi rank
5 fly a plane
6 fare
7 ride a bike
8 ticket
9 helicopter
10 bus

11 walk
12 tram
13 taxi
14 plane
15 car
16 drive a car
17 airport
18 steering wheel
19 yacht
20 bus stop
21 ship
22 road
23 train

09

9.1 ◀))
1 Tony often **goes** for a swim in the evening, but today he **is visiting** a friend.
2 Today Baz **is having** eggs, but he mostly **eats** cereal for breakfast.
3 John's sister usually **drives** to work, but today she **is walking**.
4 Clara usually **sleeps** in the afternoon, but today she **is going** for a walk.
5 My cousins often **play** soccer together, but today they **are playing** golf.
6 He normally **goes** on vacation to Peru, but this year he **is visiting** Greece.
7 Jenny usually **watches** TV in the evening, but tonight she **is reading**.
8 Abe often **plays** soccer on Fridays, but today he **is watching** a game.
9 Tonight our dog **is sleeping** in the kitchen, but he often **sleeps** outside.
10 Liza usually **goes** to the gym after work, but today she **is resting**.
11 They often **go** running on Saturdays, but today they **are shopping**.

9.2 ◀))
1 My wife usually **works** until 5pm, but this evening she **is working** until 7:30pm.
2 Jim often **listens** to the radio in the evening, but tonight he **is going** to a party.
3 I often **meet** my friends in the evening, but tonight I **am meeting** my grandmother.
4 Mrs. Brown **is teaching** English this week, but she normally **teaches** geography.
5 Hank **is walking** in the Pyrenees this week, but he usually **goes** to work every day.

9.3 ◀))
1 I normally **go** to bed at 11pm, but tonight I **am meeting** some friends.
2 Today Jane **is eating** a sandwich, but she often **has** soup for lunch.
3 Sam usually **drinks** coffee, but this morning he **is drinking** tea.
4 Tonight we **are having** water with our dinner, but we usually **have** juice.
5 I usually **feel** confident about exams, but today I **am feeling** nervous.

10

10.1 ◀))
1 ankle
2 arm
3 eyelashes
4 chest
5 fingers
6 lips
7 heel
8 chin
9 ear
10 head
11 toes
12 cheek
13 eyebrow
14 shin
15 thumb
16 tooth
17 knee
18 hair
19 nose
20 fingernail
21 face
22 hand
23 thigh
24 neck
25 knuckles
26 foot
27 leg
28 eye
29 teeth
30 stomach
31 shoulders

11

11.1 🔊
1. I **am not** feeling well today. I'm sorry. Let's meet next week instead.
2. May and Clara are **feeling** sick today. They're going to stay at home.
3. Cathy **isn't** feeling well. She is not going swimming today.
4. Jerry is **feeling** really sick, but he's still going to work.
5. We don't **feel** well, so we aren't coming to the party tonight.
6. Alexander **doesn't** feel well. He's going to stay at home today.
7. They don't **feel** well. They're not going to visit their uncle and aunt today.
8. Hilary isn't **feeling** well. She can't come to the movies tonight.
9. Lee **feels** sick. He can't come to the sales meeting today.
10. John and Diana **are** not feeling well. They are going to leave work early today.

11.2 🔊
1. I can't hear and I have an earache.
2. Dan's leg hurts.
3. Maria has a broken leg.
4. I don't feel well. I have a stomachache.
5. Claire has a terrible headache.
6. I have a pain in my knee.
7. Philip can't stand. He has backache.

11.3
1. False 2. True 3. False 4. True
5. Not given 6. True 7. False

11.4 🔊
1. I have a broken leg.
2. I have a pain in my foot.
3. I have a headache.
4. I have got a broken leg.
5. I have got a pain in my foot.
6. I have got a headache.
7. You have got a broken leg.
8. You have got a headache.
9. You have a broken leg.
10. You have a headache.
11. Anna has a broken leg.
12. Anna has a headache.

12

12.1 🔊
1. hot
2. boiling
3. cold
4. freezing
5. rain
6. snow
7. hail
8. thunder
9. humidity
10. flood
11. puddle
12. blue sky
13. cloud
14. lightning
15. rainbow
16. temperature
17. sun
18. ice
19. tornado
20. wind
21. gale
22. dry
23. wet

13

13.1 🔊
1. The weather here is horrible! It's raining all the time. It's cold and wet.
2. It's boiling here. It's too hot to go out in the middle of the day.
3. It's a sunny day and there's lots of snow. It's perfect weather for skiing.
4. It's freezing here. It's too cold to stay outdoors for very long.
5. It's a really windy day here. I'm going windsurfing later today.
6. The weather here is very stormy. Last night we had lots of lightning.
7. There were icicles on the house this morning. It's very cold here.

13.2 🔊
1. It's very windy.
2. It's very rainy.
3. It's very snowy.
4. It's very sunny.
5. It's very stormy.
6. It's very icy.
7. It's very cloudy.
8. It's very stormy.
9. It's very misty.

13.3 🔊
1. Be careful. There's **ice** on the road.
2. The weather's beautiful. It's hot and **sunny**.
3. It's quite **warm** here. The temperature is 68°F.
4. It's 14°F here and it's snowy. It's **freezing**.
5. Oh no, it's **raining**. We can't play tennis now.
6. It's very **foggy**. The airport is closed.
7. There's a **storm**. We can't play golf.

13.4
1. Spain
2. London
3. Lisbon
4. Sweden
5. France

13.5 🔊
1. There's a lot of rain at the moment.
2. There's a lot of rain in London today.
3. There's a lot of sun at the moment.
4. There's a lot of sun in London today.
5. It's really warm at the moment.
6. It's really warm in London today.
7. It's really freezing at the moment.
8. It's really freezing in London today.
9. It's quite warm at the moment.
10. It's quite warm in London today.

14

14.1 🔊
1. get on a bus
2. miss a flight
3. go sightseeing
4. apartment
5. passport control
6. arrive at the airport
7. pack your bags
8. luggage
9. reception
10. road trip
11. get off a bus
12. cruise
13. board a plane
14. arrive at a hotel

15. on time
16. boarding card
17. runway
18. hostel
19. security
20. late
21. fly in a plane
22. leave a hotel
23. hand luggage

15

15.1 🔊
1. I'm **taller** than you are.
2. A train is **faster** than a bus.
3. 79°F is **hotter** than 64°F.
4. A car is faster than a **bike**.
5. **France** is smaller than Russia.
6. Everest is higher than **Mont Blanc**.
7. 6am is **earlier** than 9am.
8. A tiger is **bigger** than a pig.
9. Your dress is **prettier** than mine.
10. 95°F is **colder** than 110°F.
11. The Sahara is **hotter** than the Arctic.
12. 11pm is **later** than 3pm.
13. An **elephant** is bigger than a mouse.
14. A plane is **faster** than a car.
15. **Ice cream** is colder than milk.
16. Mars is **closer** to earth than Pluto.
17. Athens is **older** than Los Angeles.

15.2
1. thinner
2. easier
3. later
4. dirtier
5. larger
6. bigger
7. hotter
8. lower

15.3 🔊
1. This painting is beautiful. It's **more beautiful than** that one.
2. Russian is very difficult. It's **more difficult than** Italian.
3. Rome is very old. It's **older than** my city.
4. Pizza is very tasty. It's **tastier than** pasta.
5. China is very large. It's **larger than** Germany.
6. Oslo is very cold. It's **colder than** Paris.
7. Science is very difficult. It's **more difficult than** geography.

8. Monaco is very expensive. It's **more expensive than** Berlin.
9. Mountain climbing is dangerous. It's **more dangerous than** hiking.
10. This book is very interesting. It's **more interesting than** yours.
11. Skiing is exciting. It's **more exciting than** jogging.

15.4
1. False 2. False 3. True
4. False 5. True

15.5 🔊
1. Flying is **safer than** driving.
   Driving is **more dangerous than** flying.
2. My computer is **older than** my phone.
   My phone is **newer than** my computer.
3. The suitcase is **heavier than** the bag.
   The bag is **lighter than** the suitcase.
4. This champagne is **more expensive than** that wine.
   This wine is **cheaper than** that champagne.
5. 118°F is **hotter than** 90°F.
   90°F is **colder than** 118°F.

15.6 🔊
1. 11pm **is later than** 10pm.
2. Gold **is cheaper than** platinum.
3. Athens **is older than** Los Angeles.
4. Chess **is more difficult than** poker.
5. Tennis **is more energetic than** walking.

15.7 🔊
1. Spain **is hotter than** England.
2. Juice **is more expensive than** water.
3. 10pm **is later than** 6pm.
4. Norway **is colder than** Egypt.
5. The tortoise **is slower than** the cheetah.

16

16.1 🔊
1. The Great Wall of China is the **longest** wall in the world.
2. The African Bush Elephant is the **biggest** land animal.
3. Vatican City is the **smallest** country in the world.
4. The Burj Khalifa is the **tallest** building in the world.
5. The Amazon is the **widest** river in the world.

6. Dolphins are in the top 10 **most intelligent** animals.

16.2
1. smallest
2. biggest
3. farthest / furthest
4. highest
5. thinnest
6. fattest
7. most beautiful
8. ugliest
9. cleanest
10. dirtiest
11. most expensive
12. newest
13. oldest
14. most intelligent
15. fastest

16.3
1. Sue
2. Jane
3. Dan
4. Jane
5. Jane
6. Jane
7. Dan

16.4 🔊
1. A rhino is heavier than a lion, but elephants are the **heaviest** land animal.
2. A whale is more intelligent than a shark, but dolphins are the **most intelligent** sea animal.
3. The Regal is more expensive than the Grand, but the Plaza is the **most expensive** hotel.
4. The Statue of Liberty is taller than the Leaning Tower of Pisa, but Big Ben is the **tallest**.
5. The Thames is longer than the Trent, but the Severn is the **longest** river in the UK.

16.5
1. the most expensive
2. the most comfortable
3. the most intelligent
4. the most dangerous
5. the most exciting
6. the most impressive
7. the most handsome

16.6
1. The Rialto
2. The Grand
3. The Plaza
4. The Grand
5. The Plaza
6. The Rialto

16.7 🔊
1. The Amazon rainforest has some of the **most beautiful** plants in the world.
2. Mesopotamia is thought to be the home of the **earliest** civilization in the world.
3. The British Museum is the **most popular** tourist attraction in the UK.
4. New York City and Geneva are the **most expensive** cities in the world.
5. Hippopotamuses are one of the world's **most dangerous** animals.

16.8 🔊
1. The Shanghai Tower is a very tall building. It is **the tallest building** in China.
2. The sloth is a very slow animal. It is **the slowest animal** in the world.
3. The Vasco da Gama bridge in Portugal is very long. It is **the longest bridge** in Europe.
4. The Dead Sea is a very low point on Earth. It is **the lowest point** on Earth.
5. Mount Elbrus in Russia is a very tall mountain. It is **the tallest mountain** in Europe.

17

17.1 🔊
1. coast
2. iceberg
3. rainforest
4. ocean
5. hill
6. canyon
7. swamp
8. island
9. countryside
10. valley
11. cave
12. pond
13. mountain
14. beach
15. waterfall
16. polar region
17. volcano
18. river
19. oasis
20. woods
21. cliff
22. rocks
23. desert

18

18.1 🔊
1. Would you like to stay in **and** watch a DVD tonight?
2. Do you want to go to the Tower of London **or** the London Eye?
3. Do you want pizza **or** salad for dinner tonight?
4. Is Marianne a pop singer **and** a modern jazz singer?
5. Can I pay for the washing machine in cash **or** by credit card?
6. On birthdays, we open our presents **and** play party games.
7. Do you want to go to a movie **or** the theater tomorrow night?
8. Would you like to study French **and** German next year?
9. Did you live in a house **or** an apartment when you were in Thailand?
10. I had coffee **and** chocolate cake at the new café in town.
11. Would you like tea **or** coffee while you wait for your appointment?

18.2 🔊
1. **Which** is Tom's car, the red or the blue one?
2. **What** is the biggest country in Europe?
3. **Which** is bigger, a lion or a hippo?
4. **Which** would you like? Cake or cookies?
5. **What** would you like to do this evening?
6. **What** shall we have for dinner tonight?
7. **Which** ink does he use, black or blue?
8. **What** is your favorite food?
9. **What** is the tallest mountain in the world?

18.3 🔊
1. **What** would you like to do tomorrow when we meet?
2. **What** is the fastest animal in the world?
3. **Which** restaurant would you like to go to, the Italian or the Indian one?
4. **Which** language does he speak, French, Italian, or Spanish?
5. **What** is your favorite subject at school?
6. **Which** of these houses does Mike live in?

18.4 🔊
1. My exam results were **worse** than Frank's.
2. The Plaza is the **best** hotel in the city.
3. My new workplace is **farther / further** from my house than my old one.
4. I am a **better** driver than my brother.
5. Don't go to Gigi's. It's the **worst** café in town.
6. Neptune is the **farthest / furthest** planet from the Sun.

18.5 🔊
1. My brother is worse at soccer than I am.
2. The blue T-shirt is more expensive than the red T-shirt.
3. Harry's café is better than Gino's café.
4. I am worse than my sister at languages.
5. The blue pen is less expensive / cheaper than the red pen.

18.6
1. The food in Paris is better than the food at home.
2. Pat ate the best meal at La Coupole.
3. The Eiffel Tower is the tallest building in Paris.
4. You can hear the best music in Paris at Le Pompon.
5. The Mona Lisa is the most famous painting in the Louvre.

18.7 🔊
1. Rhode Island **is the smallest** state in the US.
2. The Humber Bridge **is longer** than the Severn Bridge.
3. George **is the worst** student in the class.
4. A Ferrari **is more expensive** than a Fiat car.
5. Saturn **is farther / further** from Earth than Mars.

19

19.1
1. 8,624
2. 3,499,000
3. 496,632

④ 3,735,000
⑤ 15,265
⑥ 1,537,895

19.2 🔊
① Seven thousand, three hundred and ninety-six
② Thirty-four thousand, nine hundred and seventy-five
③ Two hundred and twelve thousand, four hundred and fifty-seven
④ Fifteen million, seven hundred and ninety-five thousand
⑤ Twenty-six million, six hundred and fifty-five thousand, eight hundred and seventy-two
⑥ Forty-seven million, two hundred and twenty-nine thousand, two hundred and eighty-six
⑦ Fifty-three million, one hundred and ninety-eight thousand, five hundred and thirty-eight

19.3 🔊
① 455,058
② 564,143
③ 3,682
④ 45,712,600
⑤ 63,859
⑥ 950,837
⑦ 23,100,269
⑧ 978
⑨ 185,794
⑩ 50,212,705
⑪ 10,460,240
⑫ 336,422
⑬ 16,703
⑭ 1,359, 607

19.4
① 453
② 987
③ 15,678
④ 28,761
⑤ 73,547
⑥ 195,326
⑦ 361,216
⑧ 548,972
⑨ 932,671
⑩ 1,295,634
⑪ 3,940,522
⑫ 6,457,815
⑬ 10,430,695
⑭ 16,852,794

20

20.1 🔊
① Sunday
② Monday
③ Tuesday
④ Wednesday
⑤ Thursday
⑥ Friday
⑦ day
⑧ week
⑨ fortnight
⑩ month
⑪ February
⑫ April
⑬ July
⑭ August
⑮ September
⑯ November
⑰ December
⑱ summer
⑲ winter

20.2 🔊
① nineteenth
② twenty-sixth
③ fifth
④ sixth
⑤ twenty-ninth
⑥ twenty-first
⑦ sixteenth
⑧ twenty-seventh
⑨ seventeenth
⑩ tenth
⑪ fourteenth
⑫ first
⑬ eleventh
⑭ twentieth
⑮ twenty-third
⑯ thirty-first
⑰ seventh
⑱ third
⑲ fourth

21

21.1
① We returned on the 9th of September.
② Sarah was born on March 12.
③ Greg was born on the 12th of February.

④ My birthday is on November 22.
⑤ I stop working on the 21st of July.
⑥ The year begins on January 1.

21.2
① is not at work.
② is going to Los Angeles.
③ is busy all day.

21.3
① True ② False ③ Not given
④ False ⑤ True ⑥ True ⑦ False

21.4 🔊
1. My wedding is on February 16.
2. My wedding is on the 16th of February.
3. Sharon's wedding is on February 16.
4. Sharon's wedding is on the 16th of February.
5. He was born five years ago.
6. He was born 25 years ago.
7. Peter was born five years ago.
8. Peter was born 25 years ago.

22

22.1 🔊
① Roberta **was** at the party last night.
② We **were** in college together.
③ You **were** a student at that time.
④ There **were** lots of people in town.
⑤ They **were** there in the evening.
⑥ Your friends **were** at the museum yesterday.
⑦ She **was** a teacher in the 1970s.
⑧ There **was** a café near the beach.
⑨ My mom **was** a dentist.
⑩ Chris and I **were** happy about the news.
⑪ They **were** at the theater last night.
⑫ Frank **was** an actor in the 1990s.
⑬ It **was** very cold in Norway.
⑭ My parents **were** away last week.
⑮ We **were** in Los Angeles in 2014.
⑯ You **were** at the movie theater on Friday.
⑰ Jenny **was** a nurse for 20 years.

22.2
① 1960s
② 1910s
③ 1490s
④ 1605

22.3

① False ② False ③ True ④ True
⑤ False ⑥ False ⑦ True ⑧ True
⑨ False ⑩ False

22.4 🔊

① It **wasn't** an interesting book.
② There **weren't** any good movies on.
③ We **weren't** in the US in 2012.
④ Glen **wasn't** at home when I called.
⑤ There **wasn't** a theater in my town.
⑥ Trevor **wasn't** in Berlin in 1994.
⑦ There **wasn't** a library in the town.
⑧ We **weren't** at home last night.
⑨ Peter **wasn't** a student at Harvard.
⑩ Carlo **wasn't** very good at singing.
⑪ Meg and Clive **weren't** teachers then.
⑫ They **weren't** at the restaurant last night.

22.5 🔊

① Brad **wasn't** a teacher in 2012.
② The weather **wasn't** bad.
③ It **wasn't** a comfortable bed.
④ They **weren't** interesting people.
⑤ Brendan's parents **weren't** doctors.
⑥ Pete and Sue **weren't** on the beach all day.

22.6 🔊

① Simon was an actor for 30 years.
② It was really cold in Canada.
③ Were there any stores in the town?
④ Phil wasn't good at dancing.
⑤ Was Rebecca in Arizona in 2010?

22.7 🔊

① Was she at school in the nineties?
② Were you at the park last Sunday?
③ Were there lots of people at his party?
④ Was he very good at playing soccer?
⑤ Was James at work until 8 o'clock yesterday?
⑥ Were you at the airport before me?
⑦ Were they at Simon's wedding last week?
⑧ Were we in Spain for two weeks?
⑨ Was Hayley happy in college?

22.8 🔊

1. Was she a teacher?
2. Was she angry?
3. Was she at home yesterday?
4. Was there a party last night?
5. Were they angry?
6. Were you angry?

7. Were you a teacher?
8. Were they at home yesterday?
9. Were you at home yesterday?

23

23.1 🔊

① Roger **watched** the game.
② They **called** their dad yesterday.
③ We **arrived** at the hotel at 7pm.
④ They **walked** to school yesterday.
⑤ Simon **worked** late last week.
⑥ My mother **danced** at the party.
⑦ They **washed** their new car.
⑧ Terry **studied** French at school.
⑨ Karen **traveled** to Africa.

23.2

① Craig **phoned** his girlfriend.
② The doctor **didn't visit** my grandmother.
③ We **played** tennis last night.
④ My sister **didn't walk** to the shops.
⑤ They **watched** TV last night.
⑥ Debbie **didn't move** to the US this year.
⑦ David **cleaned** his room again.

23.3 🔊

① Kelly **watched** TV last night.
② Tim **walked** home on Friday.
③ Ed **worked** as a waiter last year.
④ I **tried** some Mexican food.
⑤ Marge **called** her sister last night.
⑥ Marion **played** some music.
⑦ The children **asked** a question.
⑧ My dad **lived** in Canada.
⑨ They **remembered** my birthday.

23.4

VERBOS QUE AÑADEN "ED":
① washed ② started ③ visited
VERBOS QUE AÑADEN "IED":
④ studied ⑤ carried ⑥ tried
VERBOS QUE AÑADEN "D":
⑦ danced ⑧ arrived ⑨ moved

23.5 🔊

① I **studied** English.
② Jim **arrived** today.
③ My son **carried** my bags.
④ She **danced** very well.
⑤ Bill **washed** his socks.

23.6

① cleaned her kitchen.
② watched TV with her boyfriend.
③ visited her grandmother.
④ danced at a party.

23.7

① Peter changed schools when **he was six years old.**
② Peter finished school when **he was 18 years old.**
③ He started college when **he was 19.**
④ Peter worked in a bookstore when **he was 20.**
⑤ He moved to France when **he was 25 years old.**
⑥ He met his future wife when **he was 26 years old.**
⑦ Peter and Joanne married when **he was 28.**
⑧ Their first child was born when **Peter was 30.**
⑨ They visited Australia when **Peter was 32.**
⑩ He started his own company when **he was 33.**
⑪ They moved when **he was 35.**
⑫ Their second child was born when **Peter was 37.**

23.8 🔊

1. I lived in France when I was young.
2. I worked in a cafe when I was young.
3. I visited Spain when I was young.
4. James lived in France when he was in college.
5. James worked in a cafe when he was in college.
6. James visited Spain when he was in college.
7. Carol lived in France when she was in college.
8. Carol worked in a cafe when she was in college.
9. Carol visited Spain when she was in college.

24

24.1

① Carl **could** run fast.
② Brendan **could** speak five languages.
③ Sally **could** paint beautifully.
④ Rob and Sarah **couldn't** dance flamenco.
⑤ Yasmin **could** climb a tree.

6 Danny **could** drive a bus.

7 We **couldn't** ride a horse.

8 Jenny **could** play the violin.

9 Ben **could** fly a plane.

10 Yuna **could** speak Italian.

24.2 ◀))

1. Janine could dance very well.

2. Janine could dance beautifully.

3. Janine could speak five languages very well.

4. Janine could speak five languages beautifully.

5. Janine could play the piano very well.

6. Janine could play the piano beautifully.

7. You could dance very well.

8. You could dance beautifully.

9. You could speak five languages very well.

10. You could speak five languages beautifully.

11. You could play the piano very well.

12. You could play the piano beautifully.

13. Yanis could dance very well.

14. Yanis could dance beautifully.

15. Yanis could speak five languages very well.

16. Yanis could speak five languages beautifully.

17. Yanis could play the piano very well.

18. Yanis could play the piano beautifully.

24.3

1 eight.

2 12 years old.

3 six languages.

4 bake cakes.

5 climb a tree.

24.4 ◀))

1 Greg could swim when he was four.

2 Simon couldn't come to the party.

3 Jean could speak Japanese.

4 My dog could run very quickly.

5 Greg could speak fluent Russian.

6 I couldn't drive because of the snow.

7 We couldn't find your street.

25

25.1 ◀))

1 science fiction

2 crime

3 newspaper

4 main character

5 horror

6 exhibition

7 author

8 bookstore

9 audience

10 TV show

11 villain

12 clap

13 hero

14 action

15 novel

16 thriller

17 director

18 movie

19 musical

20 comedy

21 documentary

22 romance

23 play

26

26.1 ◀))

1 made

2 sang

3 put

4 began

5 met

6 sold

7 took

8 ate

9 saw

10 slept

11 bought

26.2 ◀))

1 Sophie **took** her cat to the vet.

2 I **wrote** a letter. Did you get it?

3 We **met** some interesting people today.

4 Roger **bought** a new car on Wednesday.

5 Jane **saw** a really good film yesterday.

6 I **got** a postcard from my brother.

7 Derek **went** home at 11pm.

8 Archie **made** a cake for my birthday.

9 My son **began** school yesterday.

10 I **found** my glasses under the bed.

11 Sid **felt** happy when he finished school.

12 Bobby **sang** a song to his mother.

26.3 ◀))

1 Samantha and Cathy **ate** pizza after work.

2 Katy **went** to the disco with Ben on Friday night.

3 Miguel **wrote** a beautiful song about his wife Christine.

4 Pauline and Emma **got** lots of presents for Christmas this year.

5 The kids **saw** a play at the theater with us last week.

6 Keith **bought** a new guitar for his brother Patrick on his birthday.

7 Emily **slept** in a tent in the back yard last night.

8 Pablo **sang** a traditional song at Elma and Mark's wedding.

9 Tammy **sold** her old computer to her neighbor Anna.

10 They **felt** sad after watching the film about a boy who lost his dog.

11 Mick **began** to read a new book yesterday evening.

12 Joan **found** a gold necklace in the garden while she was gardening.

13 We **took** the children to the movie theater next to the shopping mall.

14 Warren **made** a delicious sandwich for his daughter's lunch.

26.4 ◀))

1 **First**, Bob ate some soup. Then he had a burger and a sandwich.

2 My cousins have stayed for six weeks! They've **finally** decided to go home.

3 First, I went to the baker's. **Next**, I went to the butcher's next door.

4 Samantha gave me a letter. **After that**, she left to go back home.

26.5 ◀))

1 Did Samantha take her money? **No, she left it on the table.**

2 Did you get some bread? **Sorry, the baker was closed.**

3 Did you meet Rebecca's boyfriend? **Yes, he's really handsome.**

4 Did you find your glasses? **Yes, they were in the bathroom.**

5 Did you see any tigers? **No, the zoo was closed.**

6 Did Dan buy a new car? **No, it was too expensive.**

7 Did you go to the movies? **No, there were no good movies on.**

8 Did Jim make that cake? **No, he bought it at the baker's.**

9 Did Billy eat his dinner? **Yes, he ate everything.**

10 Did you write him a letter? **No, I sent him a text.**

11 Did you sell your house? **Yes, we're moving on Saturday.**

12 Did you begin your course? **No, it starts on Wednesday.**

13 Did you sleep well? **No, it was too noisy in my room.**

26.6 ◄))

1 What **did you see at the movie theater?**

2 Who **did Sarah take to the party?**

3 What **did you have for dinner on Friday?**

4 Where **did they go on vacation?**

5 What **did Steve buy?**

6 What **did Jim eat for lunch?**

7 Who **did Kelly meet last week?**

8 Where **did Peter put his phone?**

9 Where **did you find my watch?**

10 What **did Anna make for lunch?**

11 What **did you get from Doug?**

12 What **did Peter sing for Elma?**

13 When **did your sister come to see you?**

26.7

HORIZONTAL

1 saw **2** sold **3** felt **4** bought

VERTICAL

5 made **6** took **7** slept

27

27.1 ◄))

1 nail

2 bolt

3 jigsaw

4 tape measure

5 nut

6 hammer

7 screw

8 rake

9 clamp

10 screwdriver

11 trowel

12 pliers

13 fork

14 saw

15 drill

27.2 ◄))

1 cutting board (US) / chopping board (UK)

2 peeler

3 spatula

4 grater

5 ladle

6 kitchen knife

7 corkscrew

8 whisk

9 scissors

10 can opener

11 wooden spoon

28

28.1

Opinión positiva: 1 funny **2** thrilling **3** exciting

Opinión negativa: 4 boring **5** slow **6** silly **7** confusing

28.2 ◄))

1 It's a movie about a racing car driver.

2 It's a movie about two brothers.

3 It's a book about two young sisters from the country.

4 It's a story about London in the 1890s.

5 It's a musical about a couple who got married.

28.3

1 The first bank is in Munich.

2 They turn off the alarms.

3 The thieves are caught on video surveillance camera.

4 The thieves go to prison after they are caught.

5 The reviewer thinks it is a bit slow and not very well acted.

6 It is based on the Shakespeare play *Macbeth*.

7 Macbeth meets three witches.

8 King Duncan gives Macbeth the title of Thane of Cawdor.

9 Macbeth plots with his wife.

10 Macbeth kills King Duncan.

11 The reviewer thinks it is thrilling.

28.4

A 6

B 4

C 1

D 5

E 2

F 3

28.5 ◄))

1 Jo **didn't enjoy** the show because it was boring.

2 Hannah **liked** the film because it was fun.

3 I **hated** the musical because the story was silly.

4 He enjoyed the play because it was **thrilling**.

5 I **didn't like** the play because it was boring.

6 Paul hated the show because it was **scary**.

7 I **hated** the show because it was slow.

8 She liked the story because it was **romantic**.

9 He **enjoyed** the movie because it was exciting.

10 I hated the play because it was **boring**.

11 He **didn't enjoy** the film because it was scary.

12 She liked the book because it was **exciting**.

13 I **didn't like** the play because it was silly.

14 The movie was **thrilling** and they loved it.

15 I **enjoyed** the musical because it was romantic.

28.6 ◄))

1 I hated the musical because it was silly.

2 Anna loved the film because it was thrilling.

3 Tom didn't enjoy the movie because it was slow.

4 Sam enjoyed the film because it was funny.

5 Kay loved the book because it had a romantic ending.

6 Jim hated the show because it was boring.

7 I really liked the play because it was thrilling.

8 I didn't like the book because it was scary.

9 I didn't enjoy the opera because it was difficult to understand.

10 They enjoyed the book because it had an exciting story.

29

29.1 ◄))

1 Did you take many photographs?

2 Did Jim have a good vacation?
3 Did Fred take a taxi to the airport?
4 Did you stay in a nice hotel?
5 Did you visit the Eiffel Tower?

29.2 🔊
1 Did they see any crocodiles?
2 Did you eat any Indian food?
3 Did Paul sail to Corfu?
4 Did my sister go skiing in the Alps?
5 Did Chris stay in a cheap hotel?
6 Did your mom go waterskiing?
7 Did you visit any beautiful beaches?
8 Did you buy any presents for the kids?
9 Did Bob and Sally have pizza for lunch?

29.3
1 Did
2 Didn't
3 Did
4 Did
5 Didn't

29.4
1 Yes, he did.
2 Yes, it did.
3 No, he didn't.
4 Yes, he did.
5 Yes, he did.
6 Yes, they did.
7 Yes, she did.
8 No, he didn't.
9 No, he didn't.

29.5 🔊
1 Who did you stay with? **With Marco's cousins.**
2 What did you visit while you were there? **The Tower of Pisa.**
3 What time did you arrive at the airport? **At 11pm.**
4 How did you get there? **We took the bus.**
5 When did you come back? **On Wednesday evening.**
6 What did you eat there? **Some wonderful fish.**

29.6
1 Thursday
2 A T-shirt
3 By boat
4 Fish and chips

29.7 🔊
1 When did you visit Hong Kong?
2 Who did you travel with?
3 What did you eat in the evening?
4 What did you buy there?
5 How did you get to the airport?
6 What did you visit in Rome?
7 What did you do in Las Vegas?

29.8 🔊
1 Where **did you go** on vacation?
2 When **did you arrive** at the hotel?
3 Who **did you go** on vacation with?
4 How **did you get** to the airport?
5 Why **did you go** to Sardinia?
6 What **did you eat** at the restaurant?
7 What **did you do** in Mallorca?

30

30.1
1 False **2** False **3** True
4 False **5** True

30.2
A 2
B 4
C 1
D 6
E 8
F 7
G 5
H 3

30.3
1 He **has been** an English teacher for two years.
2 He **studied** English in college.
3 While **he was** a student, he worked in a bar.
4 He **really liked** working with others.
5 Gary **taught** English at St. Mark's School.
6 He **is now working** at BKS Language Services.
7 He **teaches** adults English now.
8 He **loves playing** soccer in his free time.
9 He also **loves** walking in the mountains.

30.4 🔊
1 What **did you do** at your last job at the restaurant?
2 When **can you start** working for our college?

3 Why **do you want** to work for our company?
4 Where **do you see** yourself in five years' time?
5 **Do you like** working with other people?
6 Why **did you leave** your last job as a receptionist?

31

31.1 🔊
1 What **did you eat?**
2 Who **did you go to the new café with?**
3 What **did you see last week?**
4 Who **did Anna call yesterday?**
5 Who **did you visit on Wednesday?**
6 What **does David want?**
7 What **does Fiona like having?**
8 Who **did you see this morning?**
9 What **does Tina enjoy doing?**

31.2 🔊
1. Who did you call yesterday?
2. Who did you call on Tuesday?
3. Who did she call yesterday?
4. Who did she call on Tuesday?
5. Who did they call yesterday?
6. Who did they call on Tuesday?
7. Who did you meet yesterday?
8. Who did you meet on Tuesday?
9. Who did she meet yesterday?
10. Who did she meet on Tuesday?
11. Who did they meet yesterday?
12. Who did they meet on Tuesday?
13. What did you do yesterday?
14. What did you do on Tuesday?
15. What did she do yesterday?
16. What did she do on Tuesday?
17. What did they do yesterday?
18. What did they do on Tuesday?

31.3 🔊
1 Who called the bank yesterday?
2 What did the new customer order?
3 Who gave the staff a raise?
4 Who did you see at the meeting?
5 What does the manager want?
6 Who wants a higher salary?
7 What did the boss say to you?
8 Who did you call on Monday?
9 What time did the meeting start?

31.4 ◀))
1 Who **emailed the prices to the customer?**
2 Who **started a full-time job last month?**
3 Who **doesn't want a nine-to-five job?**
4 Who **gave a presentation about sales?**
5 Who **had a good meeting yesterday?**
6 Who **didn't come to the meeting this morning?**
7 Who **started work at 7am today?**
8 Who **won the prize for Manager of the Month?**
9 What **is big enough for the staff?**
10 Who **wants to work for your company?**
11 What **was great this year?**
12 Who **wants a discount?**

31.5 ◀))
1 **Who** asked for a higher salary?
2 **What** did Phil give the staff?
3 **Who** gave a presentation?
4 **What** did she cook today?
5 **What** kind of job do you have?
6 **Who** started a new job today?
7 **What** did you buy for Carla?
8 **Who** didn't hit his sales targets?
9 **Who** does she work for?
10 **Who** sent the boss an email?
11 **What** did they say yesterday?
12 **Who** did she meet on Tuesday?
13 **What** did you tell Amanda?
14 **Who** asked for a discount?
15 **Who** spoke to the customer?
16 **What** kind of music do you like?
17 **Who** has a part-time job?
18 **Who** gave the staff a day off?
19 **What** did Dan send the boss?

31.6
1 his boss
2 yes
3 both of them
4 the US
5 IT software
6 the UK
7 £300
8 a promotion
9 her boss

31.7 ◀))
1 Who wrote to the customers?
2 Who met their sales targets this month?
3 What did the customer ask for?
4 Who gave a presentation?

5 What did the manager give the staff?
6 Who called the new customers?
7 What did the new customer order?
8 What job did Sandra start last week?
9 What time did the meeting start?
10 Who took notes at the meeting?
11 What did the area manager want?
12 Who wants a higher salary?
13 What did the boss say to you yesterday?
14 Who called you on Monday?
15 Who gave you the notes from the meeting?
16 What kind of job does Karen have?
17 Who did you see at the meeting?

31.8 ◀))
1. Who read the letter?
2. Who called the customer?
3. Who called the boss?
4. Who saw the letter?
5. Who saw the customer?
6. Who saw the boss?

32

32.1 ◀))
1 There's **someone** at the door. Perhaps it's the new neighbor.
2 My cousin wants **someone** to go on vacation with him to Argentina.
3 I need **someone** to help me with my homework. It's very difficult.
4 Does **anyone** know John's phone number so I can give it to Sue?
5 I met **someone** interesting on vacation and we went to the beach together.
6 There's **someone** in the museum who you can ask for directions.
7 Is **anyone** going to see the movie tonight with Rachel and Monica?
8 **Someone** left an umbrella in the office on Monday.
9 I need **someone** to go to the party with me tonight.
10 Does **anyone** want to go for coffee later in the café?
11 **Someone** knocked on the door this morning when I was in the kitchen.

32.2
1 everyone
2 no one
3 everyone
4 someone
5 no one
6 everyone
7 someone
8 everyone

32.3 ◀))
1 I didn't give **anybody** your phone number.
2 Is **anybody** coming for lunch with me?
3 Nobody **likes** my new green shirt.
4 No one **is** coming to the movies tonight.
5 **Nobody** remembered Ben's birthday. Poor Ben!
6 Everyone **is** coming to my party tonight.
7 Does **anybody** need help with the exercise?

32.4 ◀))
1. Everybody went to the restaurant last night.
2. Everybody asked about the new job.
3. Everybody wants to go to a party with me tonight.
4. Someone went to the restaurant last night.
5. Someone asked about the new job.
6. Someone wants to go to a party with me tonight.
7. Nobody went to the restaurant last night.
8. Nobody asked about the new job.
9. Nobody wants to go to a party with me tonight.

33

33.1 ◀))
1 Were you?
2 They didn't?
3 She wasn't?
4 Did she?
5 Did you?

33.2 ◀))
1 We gave Charlotte a dress for her birthday. **Did you?**
2 Our dog likes to sleep under the bed. **Does it?**
3 Miguel isn't from Spain. **Isn't he?**

4 I wasn't impressed with the new film.
Weren't you?
5 Frank wasn't at the meeting on Thursday.
He wasn't?
6 My parents don't like watching TV.
They don't?
7 I like your new glasses. **Do you?**
8 Cynthia didn't call me again.
Didn't she?
9 Paul didn't go to the party last night.
He didn't?
10 Chris and Dan went to the Costa del Sol.
Did they?

33.3 🔊
1 **Does** she?
2 He **did**?
3 **Does** he?
4 You **don't**?
5 They **do**?
6 **Isn't** she?
7 **Wasn't** she?

33.4 🔊
1 **Did** you?
2 He **was**?
3 **Didn't** you?
4 **Did** they?
5 **Was** it?
6 You **did**?
7 It **does**?
8 **Did** you?
9 **Did** he?

34

34.1 🔊
1 musician
2 fun fair
3 applause
4 bar
5 go dancing
6 concert
7 menu
8 concert hall
9 meet friends
10 buy a ticket
11 book club
12 art gallery
13 waitress
14 waiter
15 go bowling

16 go to the movies
17 audience
18 do karaoke
19 circus
20 band
21 orchestra
22 night club
23 restaurant
24 opera
25 ballet
26 go to a party
27 see a play

35

35.1 🔊
1 We **are going** sailing in the Mediterranean this summer.
2 Shelley **is traveling** around India in July next year.
3 We **are playing** baseball with our friends after school.
4 I **am watching** a movie at the theater with my boyfriend tonight.

35.2
1 futuro
2 presente
3 presente
4 futuro

35.3 🔊
1 We're going to France **in** June.
2 I'm playing tennis **on** Wednesday.
3 My grandmother was born **in** 1944.
4 Christmas Day is **on** December 25.
5 I'm finishing work **in** 2025.
6 I bought a new car **on** Wednesday.
7 New Year's Day is **on** January 1.
8 Pete was born **in** 1990.
9 I saw my friend Clive **on** Saturday.
10 Derek starts his job **on** Tuesday.
11 Alexander's exam is **on** June 4.
12 We finish school **in** July.
13 I'm going to the theater **on** Friday evening.

35.4 🔊
1 I'd love to, but I can't. I **am studying** for my exam.
2 That would be nice, but I **am meeting** my girlfriend in town.

3 Oh, I'd love to, but I **am going** on vacation to Spain.
4 I'd like to, but I can't. I **am having** lunch with Sue today.

35.5
1 True **2** False **3** True
4 False **5** False

35.6
1 I'm sorry, but I'm going to the theater that evening.
2 Sorry, I can't. I'm going to see a band.
3 Sorry, I can't. I'm having lunch with Irene.
4 That sounds nice, but I'm going on vacation to Mexico.
5 I'd love to, but I'm playing soccer with my colleagues.
6 Sorry, I can't. I'm studying for my exams then.
7 That sounds nice, but I'm going shopping with Tom.
8 I'd like to, but I'm going to dinner with Carl that night.
9 I'd love to, but I'm meeting my sister that day.

35.7 🔊
1 That'd be fun, but **I'm going ice skating with Victoria**.
2 I'd like to, but **I'm going swimming**.
3 That sounds nice, but **I'm visiting old friends from school**.
4 That would be fun, but **I'm going to Sam's party**.
5 Sorry, I can't. **I'm visiting my grandparents**.
6 That sounds nice, but **I'm studying for the math exam**.
7 I can't. **I'm going shopping for groceries**.

36

36.1
1 True **2** False **3** True **4** False
5 False **6** False

36.2 🔊
1 Angela **is** going to clean her bedroom.
2 Will **is** not going to buy a new car.
3 They **are** going to stay in a hotel.

4 Mary and George **are** going to visit Egypt.

5 Shane **is** going to study IT in college.

6 You **are** going to visit your grandmother.

7 Liv **is** going to finish her work later.

8 Aziz **is** going to travel to Rome this fall.

9 They **are** not going to play soccer today.

10 I **am** going to cook steak tonight.

11 We **are** going to eat pizza for dinner.

12 Murat **is** going to listen to the radio.

13 I **am** not going to eat frogs' legs again.

36.3 🔊

1 Tim is going to eat pizza tonight.

2 Ann is not going to drive to Utah.

3 We are going to visit Boston this fall.

4 Fred is not going to study German.

5 They are going to buy a puppy.

6 I am going to travel this summer.

7 We are going to play soccer.

8 I'm going to start an English course.

9 Angela is going to clean her room.

10 I am going to study at the library.

11 They are going to sell their house.

36.4 🔊

1 We **are going to cook** a chicken tonight.

2 Sharon and Flo **are not going to play** tennis this weekend.

3 I **am going to visit** my aunt in France in September.

4 Pedro **is going to learn** a musical instrument at school.

36.5 🔊

1 Cynthia is going to walk her dog.

2 Phil is going to take a photo.

3 Sharon is going to bake a cake.

4 Janet is going to visit Hawaii.

5 Mike is going to watch a movie.

36.6 🔊

1 I **am going to visit** Berlin next week.

2 Rachel **is going to paint** her kitchen on the weekend.

3 My sister **is going to study** French in college.

4 Stuart and Colin **are going to climb** that mountain.

5 Patrick **is not going to drive** to work today.

6 Angus **is going to live** in Edinburgh.

7 We **are going to buy** a new house.

8 Samantha **is going to watch** a movie tonight.

9 Helen **is going to start** her new job next week.

36.7 🔊

1 Jessica is not going to study **physics in college.**

2 We are going to paint **the kitchen a different color.**

3 Jenny is going to go **on vacation in the Bahamas.**

4 Theo is going to wear a suit **for his job interview.**

5 My uncle is not going to eat **a hamburger for lunch.**

6 Olivia is going to ride **her horse this weekend.**

7 I am going to bake **a cake for Christmas.**

36.8

A 6

B 5

C 4

D 2

E 1

F 3

37

37.1 🔊

1 The boy is going to **fall off** the wall.

2 It looks like it's going to **rain** soon.

3 It's 8:29pm. We're going to **miss** the train.

4 Oh dear! I think they're going to **crash.**

5 I think she's going to **buy** that coat.

37.2 🔊

1 Oh no, it's started to rain cats and dogs. We are going to get wet!

2 That girl has been teasing the dog all day. I think it is going to bite her.

3 Hurry up! The train leaves in five minutes and you are going to miss it.

4 That's Claire's purse. She's going to leave for college in a minute.

5 It looks like he is going to win this race. He's a long way in front.

6 The team captain has a microphone. Do you think he's going to sing the national anthem?

7 The weather forecast says it is not going to rain at all next week.

8 This traffic jam is enormous. I am going to be late for work again.

9 That dog is trying to open your shopping bag. I think he's going to steal your food.

10 Raymond is going to study science in college.

11 Shelley is not going to win the competition. The other players are all too good.

12 They're not very good at skating. It looks like they are going to fall over.

37.3 🔊

1 Kelly is going to pass her English exam.

2 We are not going to catch our train.

3 John is going to ask Amy to marry him.

4 Danny is going to win this race.

37.4 🔊

1 Tamara is not well today. **She isn't going to come to work.**

2 Look at that small child on the wall! **She's going to fall off!**

3 Jim's working so hard this year. **I think he's going to pass his exam.**

4 The trains aren't working today. **We're going to be late for work.**

5 Look at those awful black clouds. **I think it's going to rain later.**

6 I bought pasta this morning. **I'm going to make spaghetti bolognese.**

7 Mia is buying milk. **She is going to make ice cream.**

37.5 🔊

1 Sharon **is going to eat** a piece of cake.

2 Take an umbrella. It **is going to rain** later.

3 The children **are going to enjoy** the movie tonight.

4 My husband **is going to be** late for work.

5 Mrs. O'Connell **is going to play** the piano in a minute.

6 Be careful! You **are going to drop** the vase.

7 Bill and Claire **are going to bake** a birthday cake for Paul.

37.6 🔊

1. I am going to be late for work.

2. I am going to pass the exam.

3. I am going to miss the bus.

4. I am not going to be late for work.

5. I am not going to pass the exam.

6. I am not going to miss the bus.

7. Dan is going to be late for work.

8. Dan is going to pass the exam.

9. Dan is going to miss the bus.

10. Dan is not going to be late for work.

11. Dan is not going to pass the exam.

12. Dan is not going to miss the bus.

13. We are going to be late for work.

14. We are going to pass the exam.

15. We are going to miss the bus.

16. We are not going to be late for work.

17. We are not going to pass the exam.

18. We are not going to miss the bus.

38

38.1 ◄))
1. tiger
2. turtle
3. crab
4. fly
5. whale
6. buffalo
7. mouse
8. butterfly
9. cow
10. giraffe
11. shark
12. bear
13. spider
14. kangaroo
15. dolphin
16. lizard
17. fish
18. bull
19. monkey
20. insect
21. snake
22. octopus
23. bird
24. rhino
25. bee
26. elephant
27. camel
28. crocodile
29. frog
30. rat
31. lion

39

39.1 ◄))
1. Ronaldo **won't go** to bed before midnight.
2. The kids **will have** a great time in Florida next summer.
3. You **will love** the new coat I just bought for the winter.
4. Mia **won't eat** anything with meat in it.
5. My sister **will be** late for school again.
6. Eric **will want** to eat steak and fries for his dinner.
7. Noah **will win** the 400m race at the track competition.
8. My children **won't like** that flavor of ice cream.
9. Charlotte **will marry** her boyfriend this year.
10. I **will stay** at home and watch TV tonight.
11. Arnie **will go** swimming with Bob and Sue.

39.2 ◄))
1. Chris **won't** go on vacation this year.
2. **I'll** write you a postcard from Ibiza.
3. **They'll** visit their grandmother next week.
4. Ethan **won't** go to summer camp this year.
5. Isla **won't** reply to my messages.
6. **We'll** visit you when we are in San Diego.
7. I **won't** be at the party this evening.
8. Eleanor **won't** make dinner for us tonight.
9. **I'll** take the children to the movie theater tonight.
10. Fred **won't** be at the party tomorrow.

39.3
1. He'll bring some chicken.
2. She'll make some sandwiches.
3. She'll get some juice.
4. They'll make a cake.
5. It'll be nice and sunny.

39.4 ◄))
1. I think I'll visit Rome next year.
2. I don't think Bob will be at the party.
3. I think we'll go to a restaurant tonight.
4. I think my brother will visit us this year.
5. I don't think the kids will go to school tomorrow.

6. I don't think it'll be sunny tomorrow.
7. I think we'll win the lottery this week.
8. I think Simone will want to go to the theater.
9. I don't think it'll snow this winter.

39.5 ◄))
1. Look at those clouds. It **is going to** rain.
2. You **won't** like this movie.
3. There's so much traffic! We **are going to** be late.
4. Bob never does his homework. He **is going to** fail the exam.
5. **Will he** come to the party tomorrow?
6. Jenny practices the guitar every day. She **is going to** be a great musician.
7. Bob looks tired. He **isn't going to** finish the race.
8. I think Chloe **is going to** win the competition. I love her voice.
9. Peter **is going to** fall asleep. He looks tired.
10. It **will be** a delicious meal.

39.6
1. Alice thinks the movie is going to be very exciting.
2. The tickets will all be sold.
3. She doesn't think Stu will enjoy the film.
4. Alice is going to get the bus.
5. Alice will buy Suki a coffee.
6. Alice thinks the day will be fun.

40

40.1 ◄))
1. There's no milk, so I **won't have** tea. I **will have** black coffee.
2. The 11:05 train is late, so we **won't get** that one. We **will take** the bus.
3. I don't feel well. I **won't go** to work. I **will call** my boss and tell him.
4. I left work late yesterday. I **won't stay** late today. I **will leave** at 5pm.
5. I'm tired. I **won't make** dinner. I **will ask** my partner to make it.
6. There are no buses and it's raining. I **won't walk**. I **will get** a taxi home.
7. It is snowing. I **won't drive** to work. I **will get** the bus today.
8. It's late. I **won't walk** the dog in the park. I **will walk** up the road instead.

9 It's sunny. I **won't take** an umbrella. I **will wear** my sun hat.

10 There's a lot of traffic. I **won't drive**. I **will walk** there.

11 I **won't take** my books back to the library. I **will do** it tomorrow.

40.2
1 Won't do
2 Will do
3 Won't do
4 Will do
5 Will do

40.3 🔊
1 It's going to rain, so **I'll take an umbrella with me.**
2 It's my sister's birthday today, so **I'll make her a cake.**
3 I forgot my sandwich, so **I'll buy one from the deli.**
4 I like those jeans, so **I'll buy them.**
5 It's dark, so **I won't walk home through the park.**
6 It's a long train trip, so **I'll take a book with me.**
7 There's nothing to eat, so **I'll get a takeout pizza.**

40.4 🔊
1 In that case, I'll **take** my umbrella.
2 In that case, I'll **stay** at home.
3 In that case, I'll **have** rice.
4 In that case, I'll **call** you later.
5 In that case, I'll **give** you a ride.

40.5 🔊
1 I think I'll have the fish.
2 I think I'll stay in tonight.
3 I think I'll watch the news.
4 I think I'll take my raincoat.
5 I think I'll call Simon.
6 I think I'll leave work early.
7 I think I'll ask Jenny to make dinner.

40.6
1 True **2** False **3** False **4** True
5 False **6** False **7** True

40.7 🔊
1. I think he'll win the race.
2. I will win the race.
3. I won't win the race.
4. I think he'll go to bed soon.

5. I will go to bed soon.
6. I won't go to bed soon.
7. He will win the race.
8. He won't win the race.
9. He will go to bed soon.
10. He won't go to bed soon.

41

41.1 🔊
1 Paul might not come to Jane's party.
2 I will go on vacation with my sister.
3 Emma might visit her grandmother this weekend.
4 I won't be at work tomorrow.
5 Jim won't do a bungee jump.
6 Sam won't go to Spain this summer.
7 Tina might be able to give you a ride home.

41.2
1 I won't go to the movies tonight.
   I will go to the movies tonight.
2 We might go to Dan's party.
   We will go to Dan's party.
3 I won't go to the bank at lunchtime.
   I might go to the bank at lunchtime.
4 I won't buy a newspaper.
   I will buy a newspaper.
5 You might work late tonight.
   You will work late tonight.
6 Karen won't move next month.
   Karen might move next month.

41.3
1 I will
2 it will
3 I won't
4 I will
5 I might
6 I won't
7 I will
8 I might
9 It will
10 I might
11 Will you

41.4 🔊
1 Will you buy a new computer? **I don't know, they're very expensive.**
2 Where will you meet Anna? **I'll meet her at the train station.**

3 Will you go to John's party? **I don't know. I'm pretty tired.**
4 How will you get to the station? **I think Sean will give me a ride.**
5 What will you do this afternoon? **I don't know. I might watch a movie.**
6 When will you get your exam results? **I'm not sure. Perhaps next Monday.**
7 Who will you see at the party? **I don't know. I might see Katie.**
8 Will you make dinner tonight? **I don't know. I think Diana will make it.**
9 Where will you go on vacation this year? **I'm not sure. I think I'll go to France.**
10 What will you buy at the mall? **I don't know. I might buy some new shoes.**

41.5
1 Yes, she will.
2 He might.
3 No, she won't.
4 Yes, he will.
5 She might.

41.6 🔊
1 Adam **will** ride a bike.
   Adam **might** watch a film.
   Adam **won't** cook dinner.
2 Leanne **will** go running.
   Leanne **might** play tennis.
   Leanne **won't** go to bed early.
3 Peter **will** drive his car.
   Peter **might** walk home.
   Peter **won't** ride a motorcycle.
4 Carla **will** go to the hairdresser.
   Carla **might** go to the supermarket.
   Carla **won't** go swimming.
5 Ken **will** have coffee.
   Ken **might** read a newspaper.
   Ken **won't** eat a burger.

42

42.1 🔊
1 It's dark and cold outside. You **shouldn't** walk home.
2 Tim's driving later. He **shouldn't** drink that wine.
3 Clara is very tired. She **should** go to bed early tonight.
4 It's very cold here. You **should** wear a sweater.

5 Flora feels ill. She **should** go to the doctor tomorrow.

42.2 🔊
1 Carla should take time off this year.
2 Casey shouldn't buy herself a dog.
3 Kevin should save some money for his vacation.
4 Rahul should visit his mother more often.
5 Sherry shouldn't eat cheese late at night.

42.3
1 Kevin should go out with Sandra.
2 Paul should wear a hat.
3 Gabby should start a diet.
4 Barry should buy a tie for his grandfather.
5 Murat should wear a suit for work.
6 Phillip should do a language course.
7 Nicky should get a pet.

42.4 🔊
1 I have no money. **You should find a better paid job.**
2 I don't speak English well. **You should do a language course.**
3 I can't find a boyfriend. **You should go get some coffee with my brother.**
4 I don't have any nice clothes. **You should go shopping with me next week.**
5 I don't have many friends. **You should join some clubs to meet people.**
6 I want to lose some weight. **You should go jogging every evening.**
7 I can't sleep at night. **You should do something relaxing before bed.**
8 I can't wake up in the morning. **You should buy an alarm clock.**
9 I want to speak perfect French. **You should live in France for a year.**
10 I want to do well in my exams. **You should work hard at school.**
11 I'm feeling very stressed. **You should take a vacation.**

43

43.1 🔊
1 I haven't bought my friend a present. **You could go to the store on Park Street.**
2 I didn't pass my English exam. **You could take it again in June.**

3 I left my phone at your house. **We could go back and get it.**
4 I'm feeling really hungry. **We could get a hamburger for lunch.**
5 I lost my job at the supermarket. **You could work at the new café.**

43.2 🔊
1 My house is too small for my family. You **could buy** a bigger house.
2 Jamal wants to speak better English. He **could practice** every day.
3 I don't know what to do when I finish school. You **could apply** to a college.
4 They don't have jobs right now. They **could look** online for a new one.
5 My sister doesn't like taking the bus. She **could learn** to drive herself.

43.3
1 practice at home; take lessons with a teacher
2 travel to Peru; visit Buenos Aires
3 cook some pasta; buy some fish
4 buy her some perfume; get her chocolates

43.4 🔊
1 You could **buy a new one.**
2 You could **go on a blind date.**
3 You could **buy an alarm clock.**
4 You could **take it again.**

44

44.1 🔊
1 clear the table
2 mend the fence
3 sweep the floor
4 wash the car
5 buy groceries
6 fold clothes
7 walk the dog
8 clean the windows
9 do the ironing
10 dry the dishes
11 set the table
12 scrub the floor
13 do the gardening
14 chop vegetables
15 paint a room
16 mop the floor
17 change the sheets

18 feed the pets
19 do the laundry
20 hang a picture
21 cook dinner
22 vacuum the carpet
23 load the dishwasher
24 water the plants
25 dust
26 tidy
27 mow the lawn

45

45.1
1 started
2 closed
3 tidied
4 cleaned
5 washed
6 painted
7 cooked

45.2 🔊
1 Sharon **has mowed** the lawn.
2 You **haven't dusted** the living room.
3 Mike **has painted** the walls.
4 Mom **has sailed** to France and Italy.
5 I **have mopped** the kitchen floor.
6 He **hasn't cooked** the dinner.
7 They **have called** the police.
8 We **have washed** the car.
9 Jim **has changed** the sheets.
10 She **hasn't tidied** her room.
11 Karen **has visited** Peru.

45.3 🔊
1 Has Charlene mopped the floor?
2 Has Sue changed her sheets?
3 Have you cleaned the windows?
4 Has Hank tidied his bedroom?
5 Has Janine cooked dinner?
6 Has Mrs. Underwood visited Ireland?
7 Have you started college?
8 Has Sid walked to school?
9 Has she called her grandmother?
10 Have you watched this film?
11 Has Adam painted his bedroom?

45.4 🔊
1 Katy **hasn't** cleaned the bathroom.
2 We **haven't** left school.
3 I **haven't** tidied the kitchen.

4 My mom **hasn't** read the letter.

5 We **haven't** painted the backyard fence.

6 James **hasn't** tidied his bedroom.

7 You **haven't** cooked the dinner.

8 Terry **hasn't** visited the US.

9 Anne **hasn't** been to London.

45.5 🔊

1 Peter **has won** the race.

2 We **have eaten** all the pastries.

3 Michelle **has started** a new job.

4 We **have finished** our chores.

5 Dave **has kept** a seat for you.

6 I **have spent** all my money.

7 Chan **has broken** the window.

8 They **have given** Grandpa new slippers.

9 Jacob **has heard** the bad news.

10 Mr. Evans **has left** the building.

11 Mike **has put** the cup away.

12 He **has told** me about life in the 1960s.

13 Antoine **has taught** me French.

14 Craig **has written** a novel.

15 Doug **has seen** that movie twice.

16 We **have been** in France for three weeks.

17 Abe **has flown** to Paris for the weekend.

18 You **have forgotten** my birthday again!

19 I **have found** a new job.

20 Zac **has done** his homework.

21 Hugh **has driven** to work today.

22 She **has taken** her son to school.

23 Owen **has bought** a new shirt.

45.6

1 No, he hasn't.

2 No, they haven't.

3 Yes, he has.

4 No, she hasn't.

5 Yes, she has.

6 No, he hasn't.

7 No, he hasn't.

45.7 🔊

1 They **have told** me the news.

2 You **have forgotten** my name again!

3 Sim **has heard** the news.

4 Derek **has bought** a new tie.

5 John **has done** his homework.

6 We **have seen** that movie twice.

7 Jenny **has eaten** her dinner.

8 Amy **has given** me a nice present.

9 I **have put** my shirt in the closet.

10 He **has found** his watch under the bed.

11 The children **have broken** the window.

12 They **have watched** the soccer game.

13 Jo **has driven** the car.

14 Tom **has washed** the dishes.

15 He **has left** his wallet at the store.

45.8 🔊

1. Pete has mopped the floor.

2. Pete hasn't mopped the floor.

3. Pete has cleaned the bathroom.

4. Pete hasn't cleaned the bathroom.

5. Clare has mopped the floor.

6. Clare hasn't mopped the floor.

7. Clare has cleaned the bathroom.

8. Clare hasn't cleaned the bathroom.

9. You have mopped the floor.

10. You haven't mopped the floor.

11. You have cleaned the bathroom.

12. You haven't cleaned the bathroom.

46

46.1 🔊

1 **Did you go** to work yesterday? There was an important meeting at 11 am.

2 Mom **made** a birthday cake for Samantha last weekend. It was delicious.

3 Owen went to Spain last month. He **sent** us a postcard of Madrid.

4 I love the film *Trip to Heaven*. I **have seen** it five times.

5 Deena **has visited** both the Grand Canyon and Monument Valley in Arizona.

46.2 🔊

1 Yes, **I've been surfing** many times.

2 Yes, **I went** there in 2014.

3 Yes, my dad **has been** twice.

4 No, **I've never seen** it.

5 Yes, **he did a bungee jump** last year.

46.3 🔊

1 Fran has been to France many times. She **visited** France last summer.

2 David went rock-climbing in 2013 and 2014. He **has been** rock-climbing twice.

3 Cam went bungee-jumping last summer. She **has been** bungee-jumping once.

4 Jamie goes surfing most weekends. He **went** surfing yesterday.

5 Rachel climbed Mount Fuji in 2013 and 2014. She **has climbed** it twice.

6 Jim went diving in Egypt last summer and spring. He **has been** diving there twice.

7 I went wing-walking in New Zealand last year. It **was** amazing!

8 My brother went paragliding last summer. He **has been** paragliding once.

9 Archie goes snowboarding every winter. He **has been** snowboarding eight times.

10 My cousin goes caving most weekends. I **have never been** caving.

11 Ray goes windsurfing most weekends. He **has gone** windsurfing today.

12 My brother loves racing. He **has raced** in many competitions.

13 I have skied in Austria three times. I **went** skiing there last winter.

14 Tom loves kitesurfing. He **has been** kitesurfing in many different countries.

46.4

PRESENT PERFECT:

1 have been

2 have had

3 have visited

4 has been

PAST SIMPLE:

5 visited

6 went

7 ate

8 was

46.5 🔊

1 I love Florence. I've **been** there three times.

2 Tina has **gone** to Spain. She'll be back in two weeks.

3 Have you ever **been** skiing in Norway?

4 I've **been** to the new museum in town. It's very crowded.

5 John and Kate have **gone** to the theater. They're meeting you there.

6 I have **gone** to Hero's to meet some friends. See you there later.

46.6

1 True 2 False 3 Not Given 4 True

5 True 6 False 7 False

46.7 🔊

1 Larry and Michel **went** to the US twice in 2014.

2 Hannah **has dived** in Australia many times.

3 Jim and Rose **made** a cake last weekend.

④ Debbie **has never been** to India. She would like to go there one day.

⑤ Jim **has been** to Japan twice. He loved it.

⑥ I **have not tried** windsurfing, but I'd like to!

⑦ Jack **has gone** to a movie, I'm not sure when he'll be back.

47

47.1 🔊

① I **have been** to five countries on vacation this year.

② Sandra **has passed** all her medical exams so far this year. I'm so proud.

③ I **visited** Warsaw in 2007 with my family.

④ I'm feeling sleepy. I **haven't had** any coffee yet this morning.

⑤ My boyfriend **phoned** me last night.

⑥ Paula's feeling sad. Her dog **died** last week.

⑦ I'm going to Berlin tomorrow. I **have been** there three times before.

⑧ I don't have any money. I **lost** my wallet yesterday.

⑨ This is such a good festival. I **have made** lots of new friends.

⑩ My sister is really happy. She **passed** her driving test yesterday.

⑪ I **have played** tennis six times this week. And I'm playing again tomorrow.

47.2

① Rick has won five gold medals.

② Rick injured his knee.

③ The next world athletics event is in December.

④ Rick first became famous five years ago.

⑤ He has done lots of gardening and has spent time with his family.

47.3 🔊

① We have never eaten Chinese food.

② Sharon has seen that movie before.

③ I have played cricket three times in my life.

④ Natasha has visited Rio de Janeiro three times.

⑤ Yuri hasn't phoned his grandmother.

⑥ Eddy has bought a new car for his son.

⑦ Karen has forgotten her ticket for the concert.

47.4 🔊

① Can you tell Samantha about the party? **I've already told her.**

② Has Rico taken his exam? **No, he hasn't taken it yet.**

③ Am I too late for the game? **No, the game hasn't started yet.**

④ What time is Dewain arriving? **He's already arrived.**

⑤ I'll order the taxi now. **I've already ordered it!**

⑥ Has the plane from Lisbon landed? **It's already landed.**

⑦ Has Claire finished her exercises? **No, she hasn't done them yet.**

⑧ Have you done your project? **Sorry, I haven't started it yet.**

⑨ Have Bob and Jane gone back home? **Yes, they've already left.**

47.5

① True ② False ③ False ④ True
⑤ True ⑥ False ⑦ False

47.6 🔊

① I've **already** read that book.

② I haven't seen the new movie **yet**.

③ Chrissie has **already** left for work.

④ The soccer game hasn't started **yet**.

⑤ I haven't passed my test **yet**.

⑥ I've **already** visited that castle twice.

⑦ Has the party started **yet**?

⑧ I've **already** ordered the taxi.

⑨ Malik has **already** emailed Dan.

⑩ Has Terry cleaned his room **yet**?

⑪ Tony's **already** made the sandwiches.

⑫ I've **already** ordered pizza for everyone.

⑬ Julia hasn't cooked the dinner **yet**.

⑭ She hasn't been to London **yet**.

⑮ Ali has **already** bought some milk.

⑯ Has Tim phoned his grandmother **yet**?

⑰ Sanjay hasn't sold his car **yet**.

47.7 🔊

① She hasn't walked the dog yet.

② She's hasn't sent the emails yet.

③ She's already bought the fruit and vegetables.

④ She has already bought a present for Claire.

⑤ She hasn't phoned the bank yet.

48

48.1 🔊

① I'd like the apple pie and ice cream, please.

② My son would like the tomato soup.

③ I'll have the burger and fries, please.

④ My daughter would like the carrot cake with yogurt.

⑤ For dessert, I'll have the baked banana with cream.

⑥ To drink, I'd like mineral water, please.

⑦ For my appetizer, I'd like the garlic bread.

48.2

① True ② False ③ True ④ False
⑤ True ⑥ True ⑦ True ⑧ False
⑨ True

48.3

① The antipasti

② New potatoes

③ The spaghetti

④ $4.95

48.4 🔊

1. To start, I'll have the tomato soup.

2. To start, I'd like the tomato soup.

3. To start, can I have the tomato soup.

4. For my main course, I'll have the roast chicken.

5. For my main course, I'd like the roast chicken.

6. For my main course, can I have the roast chicken.

7. For my dessert, I'll have the lemon cheesecake.

8. For my dessert, I'd like the lemon cheesecake.

9. For my dessert, can I have the lemon cheesecake.

49

49.1 🔊

① Have you ever played soccer? **Yes, but I prefer rugby.**

② Have you ever worked abroad? **Yes, I was an English teacher in China.**

③ Have you ever won the lottery? **Yes, I once won $10.**

④ Have you ever seen a ghost? **Yes. I was really scared!**

⑤ Have you ever been to Italy? **Yes, I was in Rome last year.**

⑥ Have you ever played the piano? **Yes, I played the piano at school.**

⑦ Have you ever fallen off your bike? **Yes, I broke my arm.**

⑧ Have you ever been on TV? **Yes, I was on a news program.**

⑨ Have you ever seen a lion? **Yes, when I was at the zoo.**

⑩ Have you ever visited New York? **No, but I'd like to see the Statue of Liberty.**

⑪ Have you ever had a pet? **Yes, I had a cat when I was young.**

⑫ Have you ever been sky diving? **No, I'm scared of heights.**

⑬ Have you ever seen *Shrek*? **Yes, it's a really funny movie.**

⑭ Have you ever been to Paris? **Yes, I saw the Eiffel Tower.**

⑮ Have you ever tried Indian food? **Yes, I love curry.**

49.2

① Hasn't done
② Has done
③ Hasn't done
④ Has done
⑤ Hasn't done

49.3 ◀))

① My **flight** leaves at 5am from London.
② I want to **dive** for treasure in the Pacific Ocean.

③ He learned to **surf** in California.
④ My **luggage** got lost when I changed flights.
⑤ I checked into the **hotel** at 10pm.

49.4 ◀))

① We **have never seen** a Shakespeare play, but we **really want** to see one.

② Steve **has never played** a musical instrument, but he **really wants** to learn one.

③ I have **never written** a novel, but I **really want** to do so one day.

④ Esteban has **never eaten** Chinese food, but he **really wants** to try some.

⑤ Ethan has **never seen** a wolf, but he **really wants** to photograph one.

⑥ Stef has **never played** golf, but she **really wants** to try it one day.

⑦ Tommy has **never been** to America, but he **really wants** to go there.

⑧ They have **never stayed** in a hotel, but they **really want** to.

⑨ Doug has **never ridden** a horse, but he **really wants** to try it.

⑩ Marge has **never won** the lottery, but she **really wants** to someday.

⑪ Kimberley has **never flown** in an airplane, but she **really wants** to do it.

⑫ Landon has **never climbed** a mountain, but he **really wants** to visit the Rockies.

⑬ Our children have **never been** to a movie theater, but they **really want** to go.

⑭ We have **never traveled** around South America, but we **really want** to.

⑮ Olivia has **never eaten** olives, but she **really wants** to try them.

⑯ I have **never seen** an action movie, but I **really want** to see one.

⑰ Emily has **never swum** in the ocean, but she **really wants** to try it.

⑱ Melvin has **never done** a parachute jump, but he **really wants** to do one.

⑲ Pete has **never seen** a tiger, but he **really wants** to travel to India.

⑳ Patti has **never been** to the theater, but she **really wants** to go.

㉑ Mary has **never left** her country, but she **really wants** to travel abroad.

49.5 ◀))

① I've never swum in the ocean, but my wife and I are going to Tahiti for our anniversary.

② My boyfriend's never been to Paris, but I'm taking him there for his birthday.

③ My daughter's never seen a tiger, but we're taking her to the zoo on the weekend.

④ I've never tried Chinese food, but my colleagues are taking me to a restaurant in Chinatown next week.

49.6 ◀))

1. I really want to visit Europe.
2. I really want to visit the Taj Mahal.
3. I really want to travel around Europe.
4. I really want to eat some chocolate.
5. I'd like to visit Europe.
6. I'd like to visit the Taj Mahal.
7. I'd like to travel around Europe.
8. I'd like to eat some chocolate.

Agradecimientos

Los editores expresan su agradecimiento a:
Jo Kent, Trish Burrow y Emma Watkins por la redacción de textos adicionales; Thomas Booth, Helen Fanthorpe, Helen Leech, Carrie Lewis y Vicky Richards por su asistencia editorial; Stephen Bere, Sarah Hilder, Amy Child, Fiona Macdonald y Simon Murrell por sus tareas de diseño; Simon Mumford por los mapas y banderas nacionales; Peter Chrisp por la comprobación de datos; Penny Hands, Amanda Learmonth y Carrie Lewis por la corrección de pruebas; Elizabeth Wise por el índice; Tatiana Boyko, Rory Farrell, Clare Joyce y Viola Wang por sus ilustraciones adicionales; Liz Hammond por la edición de los guiones de audio y la gestión de las grabaciones; Hannah Bowen y Scarlett O'Hara por compilar los guiones de audio; IDAudio por la mezcla y el master de las grabaciones de audio; Heather Hughes, Tommy Callan, Tom Morse, Gillian Reid y Sonia Charbonnier por su apoyo técnico creativo; Priyanka Kharbanda, Suefa Lee, Shramana Purkayastha, Isha Sharma y Sheryl Sadana por su apoyo editorial; Yashashvi Choudhary, Jaileen Kaur, Bhavika Mathur, Richa Verma, Anita Yadav y Apurva Agarwal por su apoyo en diseño; Deepak Negi y Nishwan Rasool por la documentación iconográfica; y Rohan Sinha por sus tareas de gestión y su apoyo moral.

DK agradece su permiso para la reproduccion de sus fotografías a: 67 **Dreamstime.com:** Tamas Bedecs / Bedecs (arriba a la derecha). 87 ImageState / **Alamy:** Pictor (centro arriba), 147 **Getty Images:** James Oliver / Digital Vision (arriba a la derecha) El resto de las imágenes son propiedad de DK. Más información: **www.dkimages.com**